'I CANNOT BELIEVE THAT AN AIR FRYER IS SO VERSATILE AND, OF COURSE, WITH THE MAGIC TOUCH AND GUIDANCE OF JULIET EVERYONE CAN BAKE NOW . . . NO EXCUSES! *BONNE BOULANGE.*'

RICHARD BERTINET

'BAKING IN THE AIR FRYER IS THE FUTURE . . . DELICIOUS RECIPES ON EVERY PAGE.'

POPPY O'TOOLE

'CLEVER AND CREATIVE – I LOVE JULIET'S RECIPES.'

FELICITY CLOAKE

'JULIET HAS TRULY REVOLUTIONISED THE WAY WE APPROACH BAKING. EVEN IF YOU'RE NEW TO BAKING, YOU'LL BE CREATING DELICIOUS TREATS IN NO TIME.'

FRED SIRIEIX

'THERE'S NO ONE I TRUST MORE TO CREATE WONDERFUL AIR FRYER BAKES!'

HOLLY WILLOUGHBY

'THE WILLY WONKA OF BAKERS. EVERY RECIPE IS A MARVEL, MADE WITH ARTISTRY AND LOVE.'

DERMOT O'LEARY

AIR FRYER BAKING MAGIC

100 Incredible Recipes for
Every Baking Occasion

JULIET SEAR

PHOTOGRAPHY BY DAVID LOFTUS

CONTENTS

INTRODUCTION 6

BISCUITS & COOKIES 26

CAKES, TRAYBAKES,
MUFFINS & CUPCAKES 58

PIES & PASTRIES 96

PUDDINGS & DESSERTS 124

BREAD & DOUGH 144

SEASONAL & CELEBRATIONS 176

INDEX 218

ACKNOWLEDGEMENTS 223

INTRODUCTION

Hello and thank you for buying my book! Among these pages you'll find a veritable feast of delicious baking recipes that I have specifically designed for air fryers – recipes that look and taste great by maximising the fantastic potential of air fryers. I hope you will love these recipes as much as I do and learn that you can use your trusty air fryer for so much more than you could have possibly imagined. Sadly, I couldn't quite get mine to do the hoovering, but I'm working on it!

My own air fryer journey started a few years ago, when I was asked to develop some air fryer baking recipes for ITV's *This Morning*. I must admit, at first I was very sceptical. 'What is this strange contraption?' I thought. 'How on earth can you use an air fryer to produce a gorgeous wobbly pudding, silky smooth cheesecake, chocolate fondant or *light-as-air* sponge?' All I could imagine were cheeky oven chips or sausage rolls after a late night out when you have cravings and need something beige, fast!

It seemed a bit gimmicky, and I couldn't quite justify something of that size taking up so much space on my kitchen surface just for occasional crispy chips, onion rings and snacks. I thought it would be a passing phase, but I couldn't have been more wrong.

During 25 years of my career in the baking industry I've been faced with some colossal requests, but I've relished the challenge with each and every one. From making the world's first edible Christmas jumper to hand-crafting a giant ten-foot chocolate bunny outside City Hall for the global food brand Dr. Oetker. Then more recently, creating the iconic Bruce Bogtrotter cake for the *Matilda: The Musical* movie for Netflix. In theory, this one sounded simple – make a large chocolate cake for filming, then go and see it on the big screen. Not quite . . . It turned into an eight-week job of consulting, baking, and developing sponges and glossy chocolate icing that would be quick to make multiple times yet stable at different temperatures for weeks and weeks of filming. As Matilda herself said, 'Never do anything by halves if you want to get away with it.'

More modest projects, but often equally as challenging, include trying to work out how to drastically reduce the calories in classic bakes for TV shows, coming up with all manner of recipes for baking without eggs and baking when there was a flour shortage due to the awful, best forgotten, pandemic!

I couldn't even begin to work out how many hours of my life I've spent experimenting with recipes, cakey creations and sugary designs for TV, film and advertising, plus developing recipes for big-brand advertising. I pretty much eat, sleep and breathe baking! But I thrive on the challenges my job brings. I think I inherited that creativity and problem solving from my dad who used to be an engineer (thanks Dad!). I really find it satisfying, working out how to solve problems and make new creations.

So when I was challenged to make cookies, bakes and treats in an air fryer, I was really excited to see what I could come up with. Once I started experimenting and finding my way around an air fryer and what I could use it for, I was more than pleasantly surprised. My scepticism quickly moved to a creative addiction, and I got the bug.

This book is the culmination of hundreds and hundreds of hours over many, many weeks of researching, experimenting and learning. I am very competitive with myself; I like to win, and have put my all into creating a book full of tried-and-tested recipes tailor-made for air fryers that I know people will love.

I set about creating beautiful bakes in an air fryer that are no different from what you can make in a conventional oven. In fact, I'd go as far as to say that many of the bakes actually come out *better* than those made in my regular range cooker. I have found that the air fryer improves the result for breads, my favourite of all bakes. All my loaves, buns and dough-based recipes (honestly you *have* to try my Cheese-stuffed Garlic Dough Balls on p163 and the heavenly Focaccia on p158). I think it is down to the technology – the powerful fan in a small space and fast-heating speed seem to keep the doughs extra moist and soft on the inside, and gorgeously golden and crisp on the outside. The same goes for crisp and gooey cookies, and pastries come out an absolute treat. It really is a revelation to me! As if I needed any more encouragement to demolish a loaf! Early on in this journey, I amassed a small army of air fryers and, much to my husband's horror, our kitchen was taken over by different machines of various brands and sizes. Then I was ready to get into some hardcore air fryer baking and testing.

When I began working on this book, they were on every surface in the kitchen, one in the utility room, and we had three in a row on our dining table running from an extension lead. They became part of the family and each one had a name. They would all whir away at the same time, with my Alexa shouting multiple alarm calls at me to indicate which air fryer was about to go off.

One of the most surprising things I found was that all the recipes I created and have included in this book didn't very often fail. Yes, there were inevitable hurdles, as some air fryers are more advanced and better than others, and some are much larger and have settings that will allow for baking, dehydrating fruits, etc., and are all-singing and dancing, whereas some are more basic and simply have an air fry setting. But I learned how to treat breads and sponges, and found nifty hacks for making sure they would be cooked through, all of which you'll discover in the pages of this book.

I learned how to get the best out of the machines, for instance, getting to grips with the temperatures. As a general rule, I found that cakes that are baked in an air fryer need to be baked 15–20°C lower than in a conventional oven. I also discovered simple hacks that can enhance a bake, like flipping bakes over towards the end of baking to ensure no soggy bottoms, especially when using a basic air fryer with one heating element directing heat from above. Also, when adding wet batters or doughs to the machines, you need to start them off on parchment paper or silicone mats, but once firmly set, whip away the paper or mat so that the bakes can sit directly on the racks without sinking through so that the air can circulate around the bake.

There are so many air fryers out there to suit different people, budgets and household sizes – from small basic ones with just one setting right through to mini oven-style air fryers. So, as you read on, I've broken down all this hard-won knowledge for you. You'll find information for the different air fryer styles, and how to scale recipes up or down to fit in your machine. For example, if you can't bake my family favourite Easy 50/50 Loaf (see p153) in a large loaf tin, then you halve the quantities to make a half loaf or a smaller round loaf, or batch up into rolls. Most of the cake recipes are also easy to adapt to fit into your air fryer, and some recipes will have clear notes that you need to know about any specific tips along the way.

Oh, another thing to mention! Making and decorating cakes for special occasions can seem time consuming and sometimes complicated. But don't be put off as I've made sure that all the cakes in this book can be made and simply iced or dusted with icing sugar. I've included how to do this quickly and easily. However, if you have a bit more time, or if you're feeling a bit more adventurous, I've also included ways to present them in a fancy, professional finish that will wow your guests.

I've written a section at the beginning of the book that covers cake decorating. So, if you're baking in your air fryer for a special occasion, you can set aside a bit more time to roll up your sleeves, whip out a piping bag and sprinkles, and have a go at crumb coating or making a rustic layer cake.

For those of you with dietary requirements, I've also included easy ingredient swaps where possible, to make the recipes flexible to suit multiple diets. There are indications for recipes that can easily be made dairy free or gluten free, and many can even be plant based too.

If you are a complete air fryer baking novice, I would recommend starting with something basic like cookies, and work your way up. Don't run before you can walk!

It really is magic what you can bake in your air fryer. I can't wait to hear about what you make and I'd love to see photos of your bakes. For me, my greatest joy was making my world's best Christmas Cake (see p178) in my air fryer. Usually, I'd have to put the oven on for up to three hours – a massive oven just to make a 15cm (6in) or 20cm (8in) cake – but the air fryer cooked my cake in less time and baked it to perfection. What a result! Hoorah for air fryers!

Let me know over on Instagram @julietsear. Also, if you would like to see more 'how-to' videos, I have a YouTube channel, @JulietSear. Happy baking!

Juliet xxx

A BIT ABOUT AIR FRYERS

Air fryers have taken our kitchens by storm. When they first started appearing, they seemed to be geared mostly towards cooking food faster, cheaper (way less energy is needed to heat them up compared to a regular oven) and healthier. With the air whooshing around in the mini cavity acting like a convection/fan oven, it blows around any oil that you might have sprayed on the food, so you use much less fat. This is all true of course, but now these little appliances are here to stay, I think they aren't really being used to their full potential. There's so much more you can do!

One of the most brilliant things about air fryers is their versatility. While they excel at producing perfectly crispy fries, crispy tofu or my favourite, halloumi popcorn (delish!), their capabilities extend far beyond crisping up the comfort foods I love. With an air fryer, you can roast vegetables, dehydrate fruits and, most magically, bake fluffy cakes and muffins, crisp pastries, and magnificent doughs and breads.

In my view, the term 'air fryer' is pretty limiting really. I like to think of them as a mini oven, as they really are very similar to one. I think the word 'fryer' makes you think you can only cook things that you'd usually deep-fry, but that's just not true.

They really are not just limited to cooking general meals; I've found that they serve as a versatile kitchen workhorse. Many models now come equipped with pre-set cooking functions and customisable temperature and timer settings, making them super user-friendly. Also, their compact size makes them perfect for smaller kitchens and even taking out on the road if you're a fan of van life. My dream has always been to get a camper van. George, my son, said he is going to get one for me one day and I know I'll be taking an air fryer with me – no more of those gas hobs or dodgy cylinder thingies!

I'm not the most technical expert, but if you've just bought an air fryer, or are thinking about it, I'll try to explain a bit about how they work. Within an air fryer, there is a powerful heating element and a high-speed fan. When it's switched on, the heating element rapidly heats the air inside the cooking chamber to temperatures up to 200°C and some models upwards of this. One of the eight I own goes up to 230°C. The fan circulates this hot air around the food, creating a convection effect that crisps up the exterior while keeping the moisture within the food.

The cooking chamber of an air fryer usually has a perforated basket or tray inside, or multiple racks or baskets if you get a big one, that allow the air to whirl all around the food, making sure it cooks evenly on all sides.

Of course, disclaimer alert! Always check the manufacturer's instructions regarding preheating, etc. (I rarely preheat mine, I go rogue as they heat up so quickly! Especially if I'm using the basket to prove bread in), but do check the instructions and remember that they do vary. Some cook hotter than others, so get to know your air fryer by starting with some simple bakes.

RECOMMENDED EQUIPMENT

Of course, you can simply bake anything in the air fryer, like biscuits, rolls and cookies directly in the basket or on the vented racks, but if you want to get the most out of your machine and begin working with sponges, meringues, batters and more, then here are some useful bits of kit that are great to have, especially if you like to decorate your cakes.

SILICONE BAKEWARE

They are not the prettiest to look at, but gosh these are super-useful for air fryer baking. I have many kinds. They are cheap, easy to use (no need to line) and you can get all sorts online, from round cake tins, square traybake dishes, pie dishes, little silicone moulds and cupcake cases. They are really versatile.

I make mini puddings in mine, and my little round dishes are perfect for single-serve bakes like cookies, rolls and more. You can even get some that have little handles to make things easier to lift out of the air fryer basket. I use mine for baking cakes and breads as they don't leak and also conduct the heat really well in the air fryer.

PARCHMENT PAPER

Use parchment paper to line your air fryer trays or baskets. If you're baking lightweight treats like choux buns and biscuits, you may need to weigh the paper down (I find teaspoons handy for this) to make sure it doesn't get blown about.

SILICONE MATS

Reusable silicone mats are heavier than paper and so are less likely to blow around and can be cut to fit your air fryer basket. I find them easy to clean in the dishwasher too. You also use less disposable paper as they last for years.

CAKE TINS

Regular cake tins can be used in the air fryer; you just need to make sure they fit in your machine. I use cake tins in the same way I do in my regular oven as they work the same. There is a bit about scaling the recipes to fit your tins/air fryer on p15. It's best to use cake tins with straight edges and without loose bottoms or springform style if you're making sponge cakes so you can be sure that your cake layers are as uniform as possible. Loose-bottomed and springform tins are better for making cheesecakes and tarts, as they can be carefully removed from the tin.

CUPCAKE TINS

You can get half-size six-hole cupcake tins, and now you can even get round cupcake tins that fit air fryer baskets. If you've got a small air fryer, using individual silicone cupcake cases works really well, or you can also use mini pudding moulds to pop cupcake cases into.

OVEN GLOVES

I use my heavy-duty BBQ gloves if I have to reach into a deeper basket-style air fryer and manoeuvre out any larger tins or bakes. They don't look very sexy, but they are ideal for flipping over cooked bakes to bake the undersides for the last few minutes of baking.

ELECTRIC STAND MIXER

This is my favourite piece of kit. They are real workhorses and although you can do without one or use a hand-held electric mixer instead, they make bread kneading, cake making, whipping up meringues and buttercream much faster.

ELECTRIC HAND WHISK

These are almost as good as a stand mixer and can be picked up very cheaply. You can whip up cake batters, buttercream, meringues and creams, but they are not always suitable for kneading large batches or stiffer doughs.

FOOD PROCESSOR

You will need one of these for quite a few recipes in the book. If you don't have one you could use a blender like Nutribullet and work in smaller batches.

DIGITAL SCALES

These are handy not only for weighing ingredients, but for being precise when making layer cakes and dividing the batter equally between the tins. I use grams for liquid measurements as I find it way more accurate. Lots of measuring jugs are hard to read, especially if their markings have worn off.

RUBBER SPATULA

I always use one of these for stirring and folding by hand. They're good for getting every last scrap of mixture out of the bowl so there's no waste.

SCISSORS

A kitchen essential. I use mine for cutting parchment paper, making piping bags, cutting down silicone mats and lots more.

MEASURING SPOONS

Handy for many recipes in this book as I use teaspoons and tablespoons for some ingredients. You can eyeball these, of course, if you do lots of baking.

SPOONS

Wooden spoons are essential for mixing by hand, whilst large metal tablespoons are great for portioning off batters into moulds.

KNIVES

You'll need a large, serrated bread knife for cutting, splitting, trimming and filling cakes, and a small, sharp knife for more detailed work.

CAKE LEVELLER

You can buy specific wire-cutting frames for trimming off cake humps and levelling sponges. It's not an essential tool, but is handy if you make lots of layer cakes.

PALETTE KNIVES/OFFSET SPATULAS

Large, medium and small palette knives or offset spatulas are useful for covering cakes, spreading icing, crumb coating, second coating and lifting cakes off their boards onto cake plates or stands. Offset ones are a must to achieve a neat finish on your cakes.

COOKIE CUTTERS

These can also be used to cut out sugar paste or marzipan for decorating with.

PASTRY BRUSH

Used for egg washing breads, pastries and tarts, and for brushing syrups onto sponges.

CAKE TURNTABLE

These make assembling layer cakes and covering cakes with buttercream so much easier. I have a metal one as it's much sturdier and lasts a lot longer than a plastic turntable and are smoother to spin, but they are more expensive, so if you're not planning to make loads of layer cakes, then a plastic one will do. A good hack is to use the spinny bit and the glass plate from a microwave as this can be used to spin your cakes around when icing or piping onto them. Or you can purchase 'TV turntables' online that swivel, and these will do an okay job too.

CAKE SCRAPER/BENCH SCRAPER

I like to use a metal cake scraper to get a really sharp buttercream edge on my cakes, but plastic versions are good too. They are also great for cleaning your work surface after you've been working with dough or sticky buttercreams. You can get scrapers with teeth or ridges too, which give your buttercream some pattern and texture (see my Blueberry Lemon Cake on p76, where I've used one to drag some jam through the icing to create blueberry streaks – a really easy way to add a bit of drama!

FONDANT/SUGAR PASTE SMOOTHERS

This is a rectangular smooth piece of flat plastic with a handle that is really handy for smoothing over fondant and marzipan coverings and preventing finger marks. I like to use these on bakes like my Christmas Cake on p178 to give a perfectly smooth coating.

ROLLING PIN

The traditional wooden ones are perfect for rolling pastry and marzipan. Non-stick plastic ones are good for fondant (sugar paste/ready to roll) icing as they won't leave marks.

ROLLING GUIDES/SPACERS

These are handy guide sticks for ensuring your cookies, coverings or icings are rolled out to an equal thickness.

DISPOSABLE PIPING BAGS

These are available online, in large supermarkets and in cake-decorating shops. You can also find reusable piping bags, but these are often quite difficult to clean thoroughly due to their material.

PIPING NOZZLES

These come in all shapes and sizes. I always use metal nozzles as the plastic ones don't tend to create as defined shapes. To use, simply cut a small hole in the bottom of the piping bag, or in the corner of a food bag if that's all you have, just big enough for the tip to pop through. See p25 for some basic piping techniques for cupcakes and cakes. Small round nozzles are useful for small details or writing messages; larger open star, shell, petal and leaf nozzles can be used for all manner of designs on large cakes and cupcakes.

CAKE BOARDS

If you're making a cake that need frosting, especially if you're making a neat celebration cake, it is useful to use a cake board or card to work on. This helps for moving the cake in and out of the fridge in between frosting and decorating times, when it needs setting and chilling.

SCALING RECIPES

Here you'll find all you need to know about scaling recipes up or down to suit your machine, and some tips about how to get the best results from your air fryer. My mission with this book was to try to make sure that whatever machine you have you'll be able to make all these recipes in some form or other. I've written some general rules about scaling up or scaling down recipes for you to follow. For instance, if you wish to make that classic bake, the Victoria sponge (see p84), you can make this either as a 15cm (6in) or 20cm (8in) layer cake, or as mini layer cupcakes.

CAKES/SPONGES

Eggs

All the recipes in this book call for medium eggs, and as a rough guide a medium egg weighs 50g. When baking in the air fryer, you may wish to consider the time it will take you to physically mix up a recipe – in a bowl for example, it will take you roughly the same amount of time to make a small 1-egg sponge as it will a larger 3-egg sponge, so you may wish to make the larger one, bake in batches, then freeze (if you have enough freezer space). Most un-iced sponges last at least one month in the freezer, and some can be frozen iced too.

When I scale my recipes for cake mixes I always work in batches per egg. So, if a recipe has 4 eggs, it can be broken down into a 1-egg mix and then scaled up or down accordingly. We used this method in my bakery Fancy Nancy. You just need to work out what quantity of butter, sugar, flour and the like divides to per egg.

For example, a simple vanilla sponge is usually made using equal quantities of the main ingredients:

4 medium eggs

200g butter

200g sugar

200g flour

To scale down the above 4-egg mix to a 1-egg mix, you'll need the following quantities:

1 medium egg

50g butter

50g sugar

50g flour

Easy tin conversions

All the single sponge cake recipes in this book can be baked in a 20cm (8in) round tin (for larger oven-style air fryers). The good news is that if you have a smaller air fryer, all 20cm (8in) round cake mixes can be halved to create a smaller 15cm (6in) round cake. The same batter that makes a 20cm (8in) two-layer cake can be made into a 3-layer 18cm (7in) round cake, so if you want to make a taller, fancier version, go for it!

So if, for instance, you need a 4-egg mix to make a 2-layer 20cm (8in) round cake, then half of this (a 2-egg mix) can be made and divided into two 15cm (6in) tins. I tried to keep this straightforward, so for all the sponges in the book, unless otherwise stated, consider that you can either halve or double the quantities as needed.

All cake mixes work for cupcakes too. As a rule of thumb, you'll need to fill your cupcake moulds or paper cases three-quarters full (60–70g of batter). For larger muffins, you can use 80–85g of batter per mould or case.

If you're halving a recipe that requires 3 eggs in its original form, you can still scale it down. You can simply add one full egg, then simply beat a second one and only use half of it. The remaining half can be saved in the fridge for a couple of days, or popped into the freezer in an ice cube tray to avoid waste.

TRAYBAKES

There are a couple of traybakes/brownies in the book that can be baked in a larger oven-style air fryer or large basket. If you have a smaller machine, it's fine to roughly halve the ingredients and choose a tin/liner that looks

about half the size of the base of the larger tin stated. There's always a bit of leeway. You might just get a slightly thinner or thicker traybake or brownie, so just keep your eye on the bake times.

BUTTERCREAM/GANACHE/ICING

It's not quite as straightforward to simply halve or double buttercream or icing quantities to suit all recipes, but as a general rule, here are some quantities you're likely to use in this book.

Note that all buttercreams in the book keep well in the fridge for a couple of weeks and can be frozen too, so if you're making a special cake, it's worth making more than you need.

Note that if you're substituting butter in buttercream for a dairy-free/plant based butter, then it must be a block not a spread, as spread can affect the consistency of the buttercream and be runny or split.

For a cupcake

To simply spread over the top, you'll need 20–30g of buttercream.

To pipe a shallow swirl on top, you'll need about 40g of buttercream.

To pipe a tall Mr Whippy-style on top, you'll need about 70g of buttercream.

For a 15cm (6in) round cake

To simply spread over the top, you'll need 200–250g of frosting.

If using one 15cm (6in) round cake, but cutting it into two layers, you'll need 200–250g to fill the cake. You can then dust in icing sugar.

For a 15cm (6in) 2-layer round cake

To fill and completely rough-ice in a rustic style, you'll need 600–650g of buttercream.

For a 15cm (6in) 3-layer round cake

To fill, crumb coat and neatly second coat and add some piping embellishment to a showstopper-style cake (like the Candy Cane Forest Cake on p184) you'll need a lot of buttercream.

I make 1.6kg of buttercream for this. Any leftovers (you always end up scraping off the excess for this kind of cake decorating) can be refrigerated or frozen. It's so annoying when you've done all the groundwork of getting your cake perfect only to run out of buttercream and have to make more (especially if you have to make the same colour to match – trust me, I've been there!).

You can increase or decrease the cake layers as you wish, but you will have to adjust the buttercream needed accordingly.

For example, if I need 1kg of buttercream to fill and cover a 2-layer cake, and I want to add a third layer to make it bigger, I would make an extra 500g of buttercream to fill and coat the extra layer. I'm afraid I can't give specific to-the-gram quantities for every which size and number of layers for your cakes, as everyone spreads it over in slightly different thicknesses, so if in doubt, make a bit more than you need to be on the safe side.

For a 20cm (8in) round cake

If using one 20cm (8in) round cake, but cutting it into two layers, you'll need 350–400g of buttercream to fill the cake. You can then dust in icing sugar. See the Classic Victoria Sponge on p84.

For a 20cm (8in) 2-layer round cake

To fill and completely rough-ice in a swooshy rustic style, you'll need 900g–1kg of buttercream. See the Coffee Cream Heart Cake on p216.

For a 20cm (8in) 3-layer round cake

To fill, crumb coat and double-ice and add piping decoration, you'll need about 2kg of buttercream. See the Funfetti Buttercream Birthday Cake on p212.

BREAD/DOUGHS

You can halve or double the dough quantities for all the recipes in this book. Breads freeze very well, so if, for instance, you fancy giving my cute Breadgehog rolls (see p166) a go, you can freeze them on the day of baking and defrost them when you need them, but if you'd rather make a smaller batch, then just halve the quantities.

I've used fast-action dried yeast in my bread recipes, which comes in sachets. If using half a sachet, seal it up with a bag clip and it will keep in the fridge for up to 3 months, so there's no need to waste it.

GETTING THE BEST RESULTS

Depending on the type of machine you have, for example if you have a basic one-setting air fryer that directs heat from the top element, I've found that for some bakes you need to check that the bottoms are cooked through.

When making rolls, loaves, filled breads, cookies, biscuits, filled pastries and even sponges, always check a few minutes before the end that the undersides are fully cooked. For example, if you're baking cupcakes, once well risen and golden on top, carefully turn them over and check that the undersides are cooked and turning golden. If they're not, take them out of the moulds or tins (but leave them in their paper cases) and turn them over for the last couple of minutes. Once they are cooked on top they can bake upside-down directly on the racks in the basket to crisp up. For biscuits and cookies, either whip away the parchment for the last couple of minutes or turn over to crisp up the bases if needed.

If you have an air fryer with all the jazzy settings, the BAKE setting is the best one to use. It is less likely that you'll need to flip the bake over if your air fryer has this setting.

The same goes with larger sponges baked in silicone dishes or tins. If you are unsure if they are completely cooked, carefully pop them out of their dish or tin and bake for a further couple of minutes to cook through the base.

Likewise with rolls and loaves – once risen and golden and almost cooked, check the bottoms, and if you need to these can be turned over and baked for a little longer.

I even tested this with my Cheese-stuffed Garlic Dough Balls (see p163) and Cinnamon Buns (see p160). These are full of melted butter and fillings that make them a bit leaky, and in my basic air fryer, they came out a little doughy on their bases, so I carefully inverted these and popped them upside-down into another tin or on the basket lined with parchment paper to cook for a few more minutes, then popped them back into the tin the right way up for a further minute to allow them to settle back down and cool in their tin for the time stated in the recipe.

FILLING YOUR AIR FRYER

Be careful not to over-fill your air fryer. Remember, breads and cakes are going to rise, so be sure to check that your loaf of bread will not rise up and meet the heating element. Always err on the side of caution. Perhaps start with bread rolls, or make a half batch, and see how it comes out. I have some larger oven-style air fryers that have no trouble baking a large family tin loaf, but I must confess, once I cooked a round half loaf in one of my air fryers and it did, in fact, touch the element (the fire alarm gave it away!) and I had to un-wedge it quite forcefully from the machine! Luckily nothing caught fire and it was still edible once I trimmed off the burned crust!

With layer cakes, most air fryers will comfortably fit a 15cm (6in) or 18cm (7in) round cake tin, but if in doubt, start off with cupcakes or muffins.

HOW TO ICE AND DECORATE YOUR BAKES

Once you've baked your delicious cupcakes or sponges you can elevate them with buttercream, fillings and icings.

There are lots of ways to put your cakes together, and it is down to how much time you have and the style you're going for. Of course, you can keep things simple and just add a dusting of icing sugar, which is all you need for the Classic Victoria Sponge on p84, or a dusting of cocoa powder, or a simple drizzle of pouring cream and fresh fruit.

If you've made layer cakes or cupcakes, I've got a few ways to ice them, from a simple naked 'barely there' iced style to very fancy neat and perfect crumb-coated and double-iced. If you'd like to see How To videos of these techniques, head over to my YouTube channel or Instagram.

LAYER CAKES

ROUGH-ICED
(EASIEST AND FASTEST FULLY ICED OPTION)

To fill and cover 2- or 3-layer cakes of any size in a quick and easy style, I'm a fan of a 'rough' icing that embraces the texture and randomness of buttercream and icing. This is gorgeous for a simple carrot cake covered in lashings of cream cheese icing or a chocolate fudge cake covered in whippy swirls, or for my Coffee Cream Heart Cake on p216 (this is simply filled and covered in one thick layer of icing, allowing the flicks and swooshes from the palette knife to add a bit of drama). This type of icing looks really inviting and is easy to do.

It does help to have a couple of offset spatulas but you can also achieve this look using a couple of spoons. For this type of cake, adding a simple flourish to the rough icing is all that's needed. You can use a few edible flowers or flower petals, berries or a grating of chocolate or some crushed biscuits. It's a good way to ice if you're short of time. Approximate quantities needed for different cake sizes can be found on p17.

PREP TIME: 10–15 MINUTES

Method

1   It's useful to use a large bread knife or cake leveller to trim the sponges if they are a little lop-sided or have a hump from the rise. Trim these down to level the cakes before sticking them together, so you don't end up with a wonky cake. You can save any offcuts for making trifles or just eat them, of course!

2 Place one layer onto a cake stand, plate or board, and secure with a little buttercream. Pile some buttercream onto the top of the cake, then, using an offset spatula/palette knife, spread a thin layer of about 4–5mm over the top of the sponge, allowing the buttercream to come right to the edge.

3 Place the second cake layer on top of the first, trimmed-side down, smooth-side uppermost. Gently press the cake on top to secure and level the top cake. If you're doing three layers, repeat for the third layer and press the third cake onto the bottom two.

4 At this point, if you wish to make it easier to get a flicky coating over the cake, you can chill it for 20 minutes or pop it in the freezer for 5 minutes – this will stop the top cake from moving about when you coat the top and sides – however, you can simply go over with the buttercream if you're short of time.

5 Smooth around the outside edge with buttercream to seal over the gaps between the sponges. Then pile on a generous amount of buttercream to the top of the cake, enough to thickly coat the top and sides (see p17 for suggested quantities) and using an offset spatula/palette knife, smooth the buttercream over the top in a side-to-side motion to cover the top, allowing the excess to cascade over the sides.

6 When working on the top, hold the spatula/palette knife flat to smooth out the icing, then change the angle to 90 degrees so the palette knife is standing up against the edge, and using a back-and-forth motion, spread the icing around the edge of the cake to fully cover. Having a turntable for this is helpful to spin the cake around, but it's not essential. Once you have a coating over the top and sides, you can use the end of the spatula/palette knife to create swooshes, flicks and swirls over the top and sides.

7 If you wish, you can dress the cake with fruit or flowers, cake sprinkles, sweets or biscuit pieces.

NAKED OR 'BARELY THERE' ICED CAKE (CRUMB COAT METHOD)
(A LITTLE MORE TIME AND SKILL NEEDED)

This understated design is very popular for weddings because of its simplicity. You can just see the sponge layers peeking through the thin buttercream. These cakes are not too sweet as you're using far less buttercream, and they can be simply dressed with fresh fruits or berries, or fresh flowers.

PREP TIME: 15–20 MINUTES

Method

1 A large bread knife or cake leveller is useful to trim the sponges if they are a little lopsided or have a hump from the rise. Trim these down to level the cakes before sticking them together, so you don't end up with a wonky cake.

2 Place one layer onto a cake stand, plate or board, and secure with a little buttercream. Pile some buttercream on top of the cake, then, using an offset spatula/palette knife, spread a thin layer of 4–5mm over the top of the sponge, taking the buttercream right to the edge.

3 Place the second cake layer on top of the first, trimmed-side down, smooth-side uppermost. Gently press the cake on top to secure and level the top cake. If you're doing three layers, repeat and press the third cake onto the bottom two layers. Spread the buttercream over the gaps to smooth and fill in, leaving the top bare so you can hold this with your hand while smoothing buttercream around the outside of the cake.

4 Now you will 'crumbcoat' the cake. It's helpful to place your palm on the top of the cake to hold it still while coating the sides (if it's a very hot day it can be useful to pop the cake in the fridge or freezer before doing the next bit to firm it up).

5 Using an offset spatula/palette knife, apply a thin layer of buttercream all around the sides of the cake to seal in any crumbs, cover over any holes and create a thin coating over the outside. Gently spread buttercream around the sides of the cake with the spatula/palette knife held firmly against the side, and making sure it's straight. Keep the layer thin and try to leave some cake exposed for the naked effect. Rotate the cake as you work (having a turntable is really helpful when doing this if you want it to be very neat) to ensure an even coverage.

6 Smooth the buttercream off with a large palette knife or use a bench scraper to smooth the buttercream around the sides of the cake. Hold the bench scraper at a 30–40-degree angle against the cake and rotate the turntable, if using, to achieve a smooth and straight finish.

7 Once the sides are covered, use the offset spatula/palette knife to apply a thin layer of buttercream over the top of the cake by spreading it back and forth, then scrape away the excess to give a thin coating. Neaten up the edge where the top and sides meet with a small palette knife. This crumbcoated cake is now left as is, with the sponge showing through a little.

8 Once coated in buttercream, you can decorate the cake with additional piping on the top and sides, fresh fruit, edible flowers, or other toppings on the top and sides as you wish.

FULLY ICED DOUBLE-COATED CAKE

Creating a neat, double-iced cake isn't as hard as you would think, as long as you give yourself plenty of time, and ideally have as much cake kit as you can. A turntable, scraper and selection of palette knives are essential. I think it is so worth doing for special occasions and like anything, the more you do this, the faster and better you'll become. If you're covering a cake with all sorts of piping or drips, or sprinkles or sweets, remember you will be able to cover any little imperfections with strategically placed embellishments! The most important thing is to get a cake like this straight on the top and sides, level and evenly coated.

PREP TIME: 30–40 MINUTES

Method

1   Crumbcoat the cake as described above and place it in the fridge to fully set for about 1 hour, or freeze for 15 minutes.

2   Once the crumbcoat has set, add a generous amount of buttercream to the top of the cake. Use an offset spatula/palette knife to spread it evenly, working from the centre outwards, until the entire top is covered with a smooth layer of buttercream and it is cascading over the sides.

3   Switch the angle of the spatula/palette knife and continue to spread the buttercream over the sides of the cake. Use a generous amount of buttercream to ensure full coverage, adding more around the sides as needed. Spread over as neatly and evenly as you can.

4   Once the cake is fully covered with buttercream, use a cake scraper or bench scraper to smooth around the sides, holding it straight against the sides at about a 45-degree angle to the cake. Gently rotate the turntable, if using, while holding the scraper against the side of the cake, smoothing around, taking off any unlevel excess until you achieve a clean, even finish.

5   Smooth the top again, if needed, or neaten off the edges as best you can. Once the buttercream is smooth and neat, you can add all manner of decorations, from bands of sprinkles, extra piping or other embellishments.

Tip: Make sure you clean your scraper regularly. It's useful to have a bowl of warm water and some paper towel close by or do this near the sink. If you keep smoothing with a scraper that has built-up icing, it can damage the smooth surface. Sometimes, when you're new to this, you may have to scrape off back to the crumbcoat layer and pop the cake back into the fridge and go over it again. Practice makes perfect!

TRAYBAKES

Icing the top of a traybake is much simpler. You can use an offset spatula or palette knife for creating lush swooshes all over the cake, or you can add more fancy toppings using different nozzles, in the same way you would if piping onto a cake (see my Halloween Traybake on p207).

CUPCAKES

To decorate cupcakes, you can go down the simple fairy-cake route and use glacé icing or melted chocolate and a few sprinkles, or spread with Nutella, Biscoff, nut butters or shop-bought frostings, and add sweets, chocolate or sprinkles.

If you want to add buttercream to your cupcakes but don't have a piping bag, you can do so by simply swooshing on some buttercream using an offset palette knife or butter knife. To do this, spoon a heaped tablespoon of buttercream onto the cake. Hold the cake in one hand and spread the icing from the middle outwards, with the knife at a 45-degree angle, spreading over the top of the cake. Once coated, to neaten, swirl around the cake so you are left with a little mound of buttercream. Add a swoosh if you wish with the end of the knife on the top to make a luscious flick of icing. Top with sprinkles, wafer flowers, or edible flowers or petals.

1   When piping onto cupcakes you can use many different types of nozzle to give you different effects. A large round nozzle and an open star nozzle are really all you need. There are two main things to think about when piping onto cupcakes if you want to get them looking neat.

2   First off, make sure you pipe onto the cupcake with the piping bag held vertically to the cake, so you get a circular, uniform swirl. If you come at it at an angle, from the side, it's never going to be neat (unless piping flowers or ruffles, but I'm not getting into that in this book!). Imagine it's like an ice-cream machine piping ice cream onto a cone.

3   Secondly, make sure that once you start piping onto your cupcake you don't stop until you've completed the swirl, or it will look broken and messy, so make sure you twist the bag so the pressure is on and you have plenty of buttercream in the bag.

ICING STYLES

To create a tall swirl of buttercream on top of cupcakes, like a Mr Whippy cone effect, load the buttercream into a piping bag fitted with your chosen nozzle (use a bag clip at the top to prevent it from squeezing out of the top of the piping bag, or twist it firmly) and pipe over each cupcake, starting in the middle of the cupcake, piping in the centre, then swirling to the outside edge, squeezing in a continuous motion, then circling back inwards and upwards to create a whippy effect.

If you want less buttercream, you can create a rose effect or low swirl. Start squeezing in the centre of the cupcake and pipe around the middle, going outwards to the edge of the cupcake, then stop squeezing and lift away.

Have a play around with different styles, and if you're new to piping it's a good idea to practise on some parchment paper to get a feel for it before piping onto the cupcakes. Just scrape the icing back into the piping bag and have a go once you've got used to it.

BISCUITS
& COOKIES

MILLIONAIRE'S SHORTBREAD

The instantly recognisable trusty slab of millionaire's shortbread! If only I could charge that much for it! No bakery is complete without it. Make it fancy with a touch of gold lustre, and cut into bite-sized cubes for party canapés. You can halve the quantities to make a smaller batch (see note on p16 for scaling down to a smaller tin to fit your air fryer).

MAKES 16 SQUARES

PREP: 30 MINUTES
BAKE: 30 MINUTES

For the shortbread

225g plain flour

50g cornflour

¼ tsp sea salt

175g butter, softened, plus extra for greasing

75g caster sugar

1 tsp vanilla extract

For the caramel

397g tin condensed milk

160g unsalted butter

160g light brown muscovado sugar

50g golden syrup

½ tsp sea salt

For the chocolate topping

250g dark chocolate chips, or broken chocolate

35g butter

1 Lightly grease and line a 20cm (8in) square cake tin, leaving a slight overhang of paper. This will allow you to remove the slab easily once cooked through.

2 Start by making the shortbread. Mix the flour, cornflour and salt together using a fork.

3 Using a stand mixer or electric hand mixer, cream the butter, sugar and vanilla until pale and fluffy, or cream by hand with a wooden spoon. Tip in the flour and mix until a crumbly dough is formed. Knead the mixture together to form a dough, then press into the base of the prepared tin, using the bottom of a glass to level the surface, then prick the base with a fork.

4 Preheat the air fryer to 160°C. Bake for 25–28 minutes, or until golden brown.

5 To make the caramel, heat all the ingredients together in a medium non-stick saucepan, on a low heat to start, stirring often and ensuring the sugar granules have dissolved completely and the mixture is smooth. Be patient as this can take up to 5 minutes to avoid a grainy caramel. Then bring to the boil on a low–medium heat and let bubble for 5–6 minutes. The caramel will become thickened and a little darker in colour. Pour over the biscuit base, level off and allow to cool and set completely.

6 To make the chocolate topping, melt the chocolate and butter in the microwave in 30-second bursts, stirring until smooth, or melt in a bain-marie. Pour over the set caramel, level off and bang the tin on a work surface to level out the top. Refrigerate to firm up and set. Cut into 16 squares.

Adaptation

GF Substitute the flour for a gluten-free blend.

TIP
Halve the
quantities and bake
in a 450g (1lb)
loaf tin for 18–20
minutes.

JAMMIE DODGERS

These classic biscuits were actually named after Rodger the Dodger, a character from a kids' British comic book called The Beano. He was known for always trying to avoid doing his homework, but I doubt he'd have dodged eating these tasty morsels!

MAKES 10–12 BISCUITS

PREP: 20 MINUTES
CHILL: 20 MINUTES
BAKE: 10 MINUTES

150g unsalted butter, softened

70g caster sugar

½ tsp vanilla extract or bean paste

¼ tsp sea salt

240g plain flour, plus extra for dusting

50g buttercream (see p211)

About 75g jam of your choice (raspberry is a classic)

1   Line a baking tray or air fryer basket with parchment paper, or use a silicone liner.

2   In a large bowl or in the bowl of a stand mixer, beat the butter, sugar and vanilla together for 1–2 minutes until creamy, or cream by hand with a wooden spoon. Add the salt to the flour and tip into the bowl, bringing together to form a dough.

3   Roll out the dough on a lightly floured work surface to 3–4mm thick, using guide sticks or rolling guides if you have them, so that the biscuits are of an equal thickness. Cut out the biscuits using a 6–7cm (2½in) round cutter. Place them on the prepared baking tray, leaving space between the biscuits, and cut a small circle or heart out of the middle of half the cookies. Refrigerate for 20 minutes.

4   Preheat the air fryer to 170°C. Bake for 9–10 minutes until turning golden. If you need to crisp up the bases, turn them over for the last minute of the bake. Transfer to a wire rack to cool completely.

5   Put the buttercream in a piping bag, snip a small hole about 5mm in the end and pipe a ring of buttercream around the outer edge of the whole cookies (the ones without a circle or heart cut out of them) and add a small dollop of jam to fill the middle. Sandwich with the cut-out biscuit.

6   These will keep for a few days in an airtight container. They can be frozen as dough or as baked, unfilled biscuits.

Adaptation

(DF) *Substitute the butter for vegan block butter.*

Fast forward

Use jam on its own if you don't wish to add a buttercream border.

BOURBON BISCUITS

Whenever I see a Bourbon biscuit it reminds me of my auntie, Naughty Brenda, one of my favourite people in the world! We used to visit her all the time, and she'd get out the biscuit tin for my kids when they were little. She always had Bourbons! You can bake these and freeze half a batch if you wish and just sandwich them together once the biscuits are defrosted. The cookie dough also freezes well.

MAKES 15 SANDWICHED BISCUITS

PREP: 20 MINUTES
CHILL: 30 MINUTES
BAKE: 11 MINUTES

For the dough

125g unsalted butter, softened

125g caster sugar, plus extra for sprinkling

2 tbsp golden syrup

1 medium egg, lightly beaten

250g plain flour, plus extra for dusting

50g cocoa powder

1 tsp baking powder

For the filling

50g dark chocolate, chopped

100g butter, softened

150g icing sugar

50g soft dark brown sugar

1 tsp milk

20g cocoa powder

1. Start by making the dough. Beat the butter and sugar together until creamy, then mix in the remaining ingredients and bring together as a dough.

2. Divide the dough into 2 equal pieces. Roll out each piece on a sheet of parchment paper until you have two large sheets of cookie dough about a 2mm thickness. Place each sheet on a baking tray, then refrigerate for about 15 minutes before cutting.

3. Using a 8x4cm (3x1¾in) rectangular cutter, cut out 30 rectangles and place them onto the prepared tray, leaving a small gap between each one. Reroll the scraps to use up all the dough.

4. Use a fork or cocktail stick to make little indentations along the length of the biscuits, or use a Bourbon cutter, and return to the fridge for about 15 minutes to allow the dough to firm up.

5. Preheat the air fryer to 160°C. Bake for 8–9 minutes. Check the undersides and remove the paper to crisp up the bottoms or turn upside down for a further minute or so.

6. Remove from the air fryer and transfer to a cooling rack, sprinkling with extra caster sugar while still hot. The biscuits will keep for up to a week in an airtight container.

7. To make the filling, melt the chocolate in a bain marie or in the microwave. Set aside to cool slightly.

8. Beat the butter in a large bowl with a wooden spoon until soft, then gradually sift in the icing and brown sugars, beating until you have a fluffy consistency (add a little milk to bring the mixture together, if necessary). Sift in the cocoa powder, pour in the melted chocolate and stir to combine.

9. Sandwich the cooled biscuits together with the chocolate filling. Use a piping bag to get a neat finish if you wish, otherwise, just use a spoon and knife.

CUSTARD CREAMS

This is my take on the classic sandwich biscuit, the good old custard cream. This is one of Britain's most iconic biscuits, and baking your own in the air fryer, with a silky custard filling is next level. Cup of tea at the ready for dunking! I chose a cutter with a pattern on for these, but you could just use a round or square cutter.

MAKES 18–20 CUSTARD CREAMS

PREP: 25 MINUTES

CHILL: 30–45 MINUTES

BAKE: 12 MINUTES

For the dough

200g butter, softened

150g caster sugar

1 medium egg

1 tsp vanilla extract or bean paste

325g plain flour, plus extra for dusting

50g custard powder

For the filling

65g unsalted butter, softened

30g custard powder

175g icing sugar

1 tsp vanilla extract or bean paste

A little milk, to loosen

1 Line a baking tray with parchment paper, or use a silicone liner.

2 Start by making the dough. Using a stand mixer or electric hand mixer, cream the butter and sugar, or cream by hand with a wooden spoon. Add the egg, vanilla, flour and custard powder and form into a dough.

3 Lightly dust a work surface with flour and roll out the dough to a 4mm thickness. Refrigerate for 15 minutes (this will help you cut out neat biscuits that will hold their shape). Cut out the biscuits using a 7.5x4cm (3x1½in) rectangular cutter. Chill for a further 15–30 minutes on the prepared baking tray.

4 Preheat the air fryer to 160°C. Bake for 9–12 minutes until turning golden and crisp at the edges and firm to the touch. Turn over for the last 1–2 minutes if needed to crisp up the bottoms. Allow to cool on the tray for about 5 minutes, then transfer to a wire rack to cool completely.

5 To make the filling, beat the butter until soft, then beat in the custard powder, icing sugar and vanilla. Loosen with a little milk so the filling is of a pipeable consistency. Pop into a piping bag or food bag, snip a hole and pipe the filling to cover half the biscuits on their underside. Sandwich together with a second biscuit.

6 These will keep for 3 days in an airtight container. The biscuits and dough can be frozen for up to a month. It's best to sandwich the biscuits together after defrosting.

CHEWY CHOCOLATE CHIP COOKIES

I used to be obsessed with Ben's cookies when I lived in Brighton, and I made it my goal to try to replicate that just-baked, chewy, chocolate-packed cookie recipe, and my gosh these are fantastic in the air fryer! This recipe can be completely customised – I love to add chunks of chocolate into the hot cookies at the end of the bake, usually Toblerone triangles because they're my husband's favourite.

**MAKES ABOUT
16 COOKIES**

PREP: 10 MINUTES
CHILL: 3 HOURS
BAKE: 13 MINUTES

125g unsalted butter, at room temperature

100g light muscovado sugar

75g caster sugar

1 tsp vanilla bean paste

1 medium egg

200g plain flour

½ tsp sea salt, plus extra for sprinkling (optional)

1 tsp baking powder

150g chopped milk chocolate, or chocolate chips

Extra chocolate to squish in at the end (Toblerone and Kinder bars are great)

TIP
I always keep a bag of dough balls in the freezer. They can be baked in the air fryer from frozen, so you can have warm cookies whenever you get the craving!

1 Line a baking tray with parchment paper, or use a silicone liner.

2 Using a stand mixer or electric hand mixer, cream the butter, both sugars and vanilla until pale and fluffy, or cream by hand with a wooden spoon. Beat in the egg until combined. Tip in the flour, salt, baking powder and chopped chocolate and mix until combined and you have a sticky dough.

3 Roll the dough into 16 or so walnut-sized balls. Pop them onto the prepared tray and refrigerate for at least 3 hours or ideally overnight.

4 When you're ready to bake, preheat the air fryer to 160°C. Line a couple of baking sheets with fresh parchment paper if you have an oven-style air fryer or line the air fryer baskets with parchment paper.

5 Place cookie balls on the trays. They'll flatten and spread into large discs, so allow plenty of space between the balls (you may need to bake them in batches). Bake for 11–13 minutes until light golden around the edges but still very squidgy in the centre. Tap on the surface halfway through baking to flatten them, or gently press with a spoon or spatula.

6 While the cookies are still hot, press extra chunks of chocolate into each (I use mini eggs at Easter or chocolate bunnies), sprinkle over some sea salt, if using, then allow to cool on the tray for about 10 minutes before serving while the chocolate is still a bit melty. Delicious! These make a great pudding when served with a scoop of vanilla ice cream!

Adaptation

(DF) *Substitute the butter for vegan block butter. Also, substitute the chocolate for a dairy-free version.*

MOCHA CHOC COFFEE WHOOPIE PIES

If you crossed a cake with a cookie you'd get a whoopie! Whoopies are soft and light and can be sandwiched with all sorts of fillings. The combination of chocolate and coffee is difficult to beat, and by that I mean there's nothing better!

MAKES 12–14 PIES
PREP: 20 MINUTES
BAKE: 9 MINUTES

For the batter

150g dark chocolate

100g salted butter

125g self-raising flour

25g cocoa powder

2 medium eggs

100g light muscovado sugar

2 tbsp strong coffee (instant espresso powder and water)

3–4 tbsp milk

For the filling

60g unsalted butter, at room temperature

40g full-fat cream cheese, at room temperature

120g icing sugar, sifted

2 tsp strong coffee, or a shot of Baileys or whisky

1 Line the air fryer baking trays with parchment paper or silicone liners as the batter is very wet.

2 Start by making the batter. Melt the chocolate and butter in a bain-marie, or in the microwave on a medium heat in 30-second bursts, stirring between bursts until combined.

3 In a separate bowl, mix the flour and cocoa powder together.

4 In another bowl, whisk the eggs and sugar for 1–2 minutes on high with an electric whisk until pale, thick and a ribbon trail appears when the whisk is lifted. Add the melted chocolate and butter, then whisk for 1 minute on high. Add the coffee and whisk to mix thoroughly. Fold in the flour mixture and loosen with the milk. The batter should be sticky and a peanut butter consistency.

5 Using two spoons or an ice-cream scoop, place dollops of batter on the prepared trays, leaving space between for spreading. Smooth over the tops with damp fingers.

6 Preheat the air fryer to 160°C. Bake for 7–9 minutes. After 4 minutes, tap the trays or press the pies down gently with a rubber spatula to flatten. Continue baking until just crisp around the edges and set over on the tops. The pies should be underbaked a little more than you're comfortable with, fudge-like and very squidgy as they will set as they cool. Leave to cool on the tray.

7 Meanwhile, make the filling. Beat the butter and cream cheese until smooth and creamy, then beat in the icing sugar until very pale and fluffy. Gently stir through the coffee until combined. Pipe or spoon the filling onto an upturned cookie and sandwich with a second to create whoopie pies.

Adaptation

(GF) *Substitute the flour for a gluten-free blend.*

TIP
Best eaten fresh, or store in the fridge in an airtight container for up to 3 days. Bring to room temperature to serve.

OATY RAISIN COOKIES

These flavour-packed hearty cookies are soft, chewy and full of oats, so they are great for an energy pick-me-up or for lunch boxes. The oats and use of oil instead of butter make this one of my healthier recipes.

MAKES 14–16 COOKIES
PREP: 15 MINUTES
BAKE: 15 MINUTES

125g raisins

50g boiling water

150g sunflower oil, olive oil or melted coconut oil

175g golden caster sugar

1 medium egg

1 tsp ground cinnamon

1 tsp vanilla extract

130g self-raising flour

¼ tsp bicarbonate of soda

¼ tsp sea salt

300g oats

1 Line a baking tray with parchment paper, or use a silicone liner.

2 Put the raisins in a small bowl and pour over the boiling water. Soak for 20 minutes until plump.

3 Meanwhile, in a large bowl, mix the oil and sugar together. Gradually beat in the egg, along with the reserved water from the raisins, the cinnamon and vanilla. Sift in the flour, bicarbonate of soda and salt, then add the oats. Stir well, then mix in the plumped-up raisins. Drop heaped tablespoons of the dough onto the prepared baking tray, making sure they are well spaced apart as the cookies will spread when cooking.

4 Preheat the air fryer to 160°C. Bake for 12–15 minutes until golden. Press them down gently halfway through the bake to flatten them a little. Leave to cool on the tray for 10 minutes before tucking in, or transfer to a wire rack to cool completely.

5 These cookies will keep in an airtight container for up to 3 days, or they can be frozen.

Adaptations

(GF) *Substitute the flour for a gluten-free blend. Also, make sure the oats are gluten free.*

(PB) *Substitute the egg for flax egg (see Tip on p83).*

TIP
Uncooked dough can be rolled into balls, flattened and frozen for baking fresh in the air fryer any time you want a warm oat cookie. Just bake for a few more minutes.

FLAPJACKS

These are a great idea for using up store cupboard cereals. I don't know anyone who doesn't have boxes or bags of unused cereal hanging around in their cupboard, just waiting for the day when they're too stale to eat and end up in the bin. You could even mix and match your favourite cereals! Flapjacks send me straight back to my childhood as they were one of the very first things I ever baked. They are pretty fool proof, so a really quick and easy bake, but so satisfying!

**MAKES ABOUT
16 SQUARES**
PREP: 15 MINUTES
BAKE: 12 MINUTES

75g oats

75g cornflakes

75g Rice Krispies

150g butter, plus extra for greasing

90g sugar

75g golden syrup, maple syrup or honey

1 Grease and line a 23cm (9in) square cake tin with parchment paper.

2 Combine the oats and cereals in a bowl.

3 In a non-stick saucepan large enough to hold the cereals, gently heat the butter, sugar and syrup together on a low–medium heat until the sugar has dissolved and you have a warm, smooth liquid. Remove from the heat.

4 Tip in the cereals and use a wooden spoon or spatula to fold through the cereals, making sure they are coated in the sugar mixture. Pour into the prepared tin and use a spatula to flatten and pack down the cereal.

5 Preheat the air fryer to 170°C. Bake for 10–12 minutes until lightly golden and bubbly. Leave to cool in the tin completely, then remove and cut into squares. These will keep for about 2 weeks if well wrapped.

Adaptation

(DF) Substitute the butter for vegan block butter or spread.

TIP
You can use small individual silicone moulds if you prefer. Press the cereal down into the moulds using the back of a spoon. Bake for 8–9 minutes.

SLICE-AND-BAKE CHOCOLATE AND HAZELNUT FREEZER COOKIES

If you love a freshly baked treat but don't want to get the rolling pin out every time you fancy a nibble, these cookies are for you! This pre-made cookie dough is simple and delicious, but the best thing is you can store it in the fridge or freezer and just slice and bake whenever you're feeling peckish. Allow to soften at room temperature a little if slicing from frozen, then pop back in the freezer.

MAKES 12–16 COOKIES

PREP: 15 MINUTES
CHILL: 1 HOUR
BAKE: 12 MINUTES

220g plain flour

50g unsweetened cocoa powder

¼ tsp baking powder

½ tsp sea salt

125g unsalted butter, at room temperature

100g light muscovado sugar

2 tsp vanilla extract or bean paste

1 medium egg

75g hazelnuts, toasted and finely chopped

TIPS
• Switch the hazelnuts for pistachios, peanuts or almonds.
• Toast hazelnuts in the air fryer at 150°C. Use a small dish covered in foil so that the nuts don't get blown about!

1   Line a baking tray with parchment paper, or use a silicone liner.

2   Put the flour in a bowl and whisk in the cocoa powder, baking powder and salt.

3   In a separate large bowl, beat the butter, sugar and vanilla together until combined. Beat in the egg. Slowly mix in the dry ingredients and 25g of the nuts. Lay the rest of the nuts out onto a clean work surface.

4   Shape the mixture into a chubby log, approx 5cm in diameter (or if you prefer smaller cookies, make two logs), then gently roll over the nuts to encrust the surface. Wrap tightly in clingfilm, twisting at the ends, and chill for at least 1 hour before slicing and baking. You can freeze them all at this stage and bake however many you need in the air fryer in batches. They will need an extra 2 minutes if baked from frozen.

5   Preheat the air fryer to 160°C. Place the cookies on the prepared tray, leaving space between each one as they will spread out. Bake for 10–12 minutes. Allow to firm up on the tray for 5 minutes, then transfer to a wire rack to cool. Serve warm or at room temperature. These keep for up to 5 days in an airtight container.

Adaptation
(DF) Substitute the butter for vegan block butter.

STRAWBERRIES AND CREAM SHORTBREAD STACKS

These treats are perfect for adorning the table for afternoon tea. They look really fancy, with three thin biscuits sandwiching slices of strawberry and dollops of fresh whipped cream. These always make me think of the world of Strawberry Shortcake, which unless you were around in the '80s like me, you might need to Google! These stacks are simple to make but look so effective. Best served around Wimbledon, but not with a tennis racket!

MAKES 6–8 STACKS
PREP: 20 MINUTES
BAKE: 12 MINUTES

For the biscuits

140g unsalted butter, softened

60g caster sugar, plus 1 tsp for sprinkling

½ tsp vanilla extract or bean paste

225g plain flour, plus extra for dusting

¼ tsp sea salt

For the filling

200g double cream

1 tbsp icing sugar, plus extra for dusting

1 tsp vanilla extract or bean paste

About 250g strawberries, chopped into small pieces

1   Line a baking tray with parchment paper, or use a silicone liner.

2   Start by making the biscuits. Beat the butter, sugar and vanilla together to just combine (do not overmix or the biscuits will spread when cooking). Add the flour and salt, mixing together until the mixture starts to resemble chunky breadcrumbs. Once again, do not overmix as you want the stacks to be short and crumbly.

3   Tip the dough onto a work surface and bring together, briefly kneading, then pat down into a circle. Dust the surface with a little flour and pop the dough on top of the flour. Dust the top of the dough and a rolling pin. Roll out to a 3–4mm (¼in) thickness, turning every so often and dusting with flour if you need to, to prevent sticking. Prick a few times with a fork. Cut out 18–24 circles using a 7cm (2½in) round fluted cutter and place on the prepared tray, leaving a little space between each.

4   Preheat the air fryer to 160°C. Bake for 10–12 minutes until golden. Sprinkle a little caster sugar over the warm biscuits and leave to cool on the tray for 5 minutes before transferring to a wire rack to cool completely.

5   To make the filling, gently whip the cream, icing sugar and vanilla together to soft peaks.

6   Pipe or spoon a layer of cream over one biscuit, then add a layer of strawberries. Top with a second biscuit and repeat with the cream and strawberries, then top with the third and final biscuit. Dust with a little icing sugar before serving.

Adaptation

(DF) *Substitute the butter for vegan block butter and use dairy-free plant-based cream.*

VIENNESE WHIRLS

These delicate buttery biscuits are totally scrumptious served plain, dipped in chocolate or sandwiched. I make these in a few different flavours so there's something for everyone: jam and buttercream; half chocolate dipped; or sandwiched with chocolate filling. These were favoured in my family growing up: they would often cause a fight with my sister over who had the last one! Every time I eat these, that melt-in-the-mouth biscuit transports me right back there!

MAKES ABOUT 22–24 WHIRLS
PREP: 30 MINUTES
CHILL: 30 MINUTES
BAKE: 15 MINUTES

For the biscuits

250g unsalted butter, very soft

50g icing sugar

1 tsp vanilla extract or bean paste

220g plain flour

60g cornflour

½ tsp sea salt

For the chocolate dip

Dark, milk or white chocolate (about 150g in total in small bowls)

For the filling

Strawberry jam

100g unsalted butter, softened

½ tsp vanilla extract

200g icing sugar, plus extra for dusting

A little milk, to loosen

1   Using a 5cm (2in) round cutter as a guide, draw well-spaced-apart circles on a sheet of parchment paper the size of the tray that will fit in your air fryer. Turn the paper over.

2   Start by making the biscuits. Put the butter, sugar and vanilla in a bowl and beat until pale and fluffy. Sift in the flour, cornflour and salt and beat until thoroughly mixed, but don't overmix. Spoon the mixture into a piping bag fitted with a large open star nozzle (I used a 1M). Pipe the shapes onto the parchment paper. For circles, pipe swirled rounds inside the templates.

3   Ideally, chill for 20–30 minutes in the fridge or in the freezer for 15 minutes – they will keep their shape better. Otherwise they can be baked straight away, but they will lose a little definition. You can also freeze them all at this stage and bake however many you need in the air fryer in batches. They will need an extra 2 minutes if baked from frozen.

4   Preheat the air fryer to 160°C. Bake for 12–15 minutes until as golden as you like. Remove the parchment paper to crisp up the bottoms for the last 2 minutes. Cool on the tray for 5 minutes, then carefully transfer to a wire rack to cool completely.

5   If you like the biscuits with chocolate, melt the chocolate in a bain-marie and dip in a third of the way, then set on parchment paper to dry. Alternatively, sandwich with jam and buttercream.

6   To make the buttercream, beat the butter and vanilla together, then gradually beat in the icing sugar until pale, creamy and fluffy. Loosen with a little milk to make a spreadable consistency. It looks lovely to pipe the buttercream with a small star nozzle (I used a Jem 30) to replicate the swirls on the biscuits if you want to be fancy, but you can of course just use a knife or spoon to fill if you prefer.

Adaptation

(DF) *Substitute the butter for vegan block butter. Also, substitute the chocolate for a dairy-free version.*

SALTED CARAMEL-STUFFED COOKIES

These cookies are delicious on their own or served with a scoop of ice cream as a pudding. I keep a handy little (okay, large) bag of these uncooked in the freezer so you can air fry them whenever someone fancies a warm cookie, usually when we're having a cosy movie night in! (Also great for enticing buyers when you're trying to sell your house.)

MAKES 12–14 COOKIES

PREP: 15 MINUTES
CHILL: 30 MINUTES
BAKE: 12 MINUTES

160g self-raising flour

25g cocoa powder

¼ tsp fine sea salt

125g unsalted butter, softened

75g light brown sugar

75g golden caster sugar

1 medium egg

1 tsp vanilla extract

150g dark chocolate chips or chopped chocolate

Salted caramel sweets (I used Werther's Salted Caramel Cream), refrigerated

Sea salt flakes, for sprinkling (optional)

1   Line a baking tray with parchment paper, or use a silicone liner.

2   Put the flour in a bowl and stir in the cocoa powder and salt.

3   In a separate bowl, cream the butter and both sugars together until pale and fluffy, then beat in the egg and vanilla. Stir in the flour mix and the chocolate chips until you get a dough-like consistency.

4   Make balls of cookie dough (I weigh mine so they are the same size – 45g each), using slightly damp hands to avoid sticking.

5   Get stuffing! Flatten each ball slightly in the palm of your hand and press in a chilled sweet, then form into a ball again. Refrigerate for about 30 minutes (this can be done the day before, or frozen at this point).

6   Preheat the air fryer to 160°C. Place the cookies on the prepared tray, leaving space between each as they will spread out. Sprinkle with sea salt flakes, if using. Bake for 10–12 minutes, gently pressing down with a silicone spatula to help flatten halfway through the bake. Bake until firm at the edges but still soft and gooey in the middle – they will firm up a little as they cool, so don't be tempted to overbake them. If baking from frozen, they will need an extra 1–2 minutes.

7   Leave to cool on the tray, then transfer to a wire rack to cool completely. Best served warm so the caramel is melty.

FUNFETTI COOKIES

These deliciously soft and chewy cookies are best served warm straight out of the oven with a side of ice cream! They'll keep in an airtight container or food bag for up to a week, and you can refresh them in an air fryer at 140°C for a couple of minutes. Not to be thrown at weddings.

MAKES 26–28 COOKIES

PREP: 15 MINUTES
CHILL: 1 HOUR
BAKE: 12 MINUTES

175g unsalted butter, softened

175g golden caster sugar

120g light muscovado sugar

2 tsp vanilla extract or bean paste

1 medium egg

½ tsp sea salt (optional)

100g Funfetti or bright cake sprinkles (ensure they are bake stable)

375g plain flour

1   Line a baking tray with parchment paper, or use a silicone liner.

2   Beat the butter, both sugars and vanilla until creamy. Add the egg and mix until combined. Add the salt, if using, 30g of the sprinkles and the flour, and mix to form a dough.

3   Roll the dough into one large log about 6cm (2in) in diameter (or split the dough in half to make two smaller logs, if you prefer).

4   Spread the remaining sprinkles onto a clean work surface and roll the log into the sprinkles to encrust the surface. Roll up tightly in clingfilm and chill for at least 1 hour before slicing and baking. If you like, you can freeze the dough now for later use.

5   Remove the log from the fridge and allow to soften a little so it is easier to slice. Slice into 8mm (¼in) thick rounds, and place onto the prepared tray or pop directly into the baskets, leaving enough space between the cookies as they will spread.

6   Preheat the air fryer to 160°C. Bake for 10–12 minutes until the tops feel sandy and firm to the touch but still squidgy in the middle. Don't be tempted to overbake as they will firm up as they cool.

7   Remove from the air fryer, leave to firm up for 5–10 minutes, then transfer to a wire rack to cool completely.

Adaptation

(DF) *Substitute the butter for vegan block butter.*

PARTY RINGS

A children's party wouldn't be a children's party without them! These colourful biscuits just refuse to date and seeing a big plateful of them as a child always made me happy. They are traditionally fairly pastel, but I love going OTT and using neon and bright shades! A fluted paper doily on the plate first is optional.

MAKES ABOUT 16 RINGS
PREP: 30 MINUTES
CHILL: 15 MINUTES
BAKE: 10 MINUTES
SETTING: 2 HOURS

For the biscuits

200g plain flour, plus extra for dusting

½ tsp sea salt

30g cornflour

100g unsalted butter, softened

1 tsp vanilla extract

100g caster sugar

1 medium egg

For the royal icing

300g icing sugar

Juice of 1 lemon

1 egg white

Gel food colourings of your choice

1 Line a baking tray with parchment paper, or use a silicone liner.

2 Start by making the biscuits. Dry mix the flour, salt and cornflour together.

3 Beat the butter, vanilla and sugar together in a stand mixer or with a wooden spoon until combined, but not pale and creamy, or the biscuits will spread. Beat in the egg. Tip in the flour mixture and knead into a dough. If doing this by hand, briefly knead once all combined to make a smooth and rollable dough.

4 Lightly dust a work surface and roll out the dough to a 5–6mm (¼in) thickness. Use guide sticks, if you have them. Flour a 7cm (3in) round cutter and stamp out 12 circles, re-rolling the dough to use up the scraps. Transfer to the prepared tray and refrigerate for at least 15 minutes before baking. If baking in baskets, put the biscuits on individual pieces of parchment paper, ready to be dropped into the baskets, then cut out the centre of each biscuit using a 2½ cm (1in) round cutter.

5 Preheat the air fryer to 160°C. Bake for 8–10 minutes until light golden. Allow to cool for 5 minutes on the tray, then transfer to a wire rack to cool completely.

6 Meanwhile, make the icing. Put the icing sugar, lemon juice and egg white in a bowl and stir until you have a smooth icing with a flooding consistency (or use royal icing sugar and add water, if you prefer, and follow packet instructions). Keep 2 tablespoons of the icing white, transfer it to a piping bag and set aside. This will be used the create the decorative lines.

7 Divide the rest of the icing between four small bowls (large enough for you to dip the biscuits onto the surface of the icing but not so big that the icing is too shallow) and colour each with food colourings.

recipe continued overleaf . . .

8   Place a biscuit onto the surface of the icing in the bowl, allowing the top to become covered with icing, but not dripping over the edge. Lift it up off the icing and use the side of the bowl or spoon to gently scrape off any excess icing. Give the biscuit a shake to settle the icing and pop onto a wire rack, icing-side up. Repeat with the other biscuits.

9   Snip a 3mm hole in the white icing piping bag and pipe thin, straight lines over the biscuits in one direction, then use a cocktail stick to create a feathered effect by dragging through the icing across the lines.

10 Allow to set for a couple of hours. Once dried they will keep for up to a week in an airtight container.

Adaptation

(DF) *Substitute the butter for vegan block butter.*

Fast Forward

Use royal icing sugar and add water, according to packet instructions, rather than making royal icing from scratch.

TIP
You may need to add the lines after dunking a few biscuits, as the icing does start to dry out after a few minutes. Adding lines as you go will prevent the icing from setting too much before dragging through the white feathered effect.

THUMB PRINT COOKIES

Iconic thumb print cookies! These are so easy to make, and great fun to bake with kids. The lovely thing about these cookies is that they are pretty much a sweet and crispy receptacle for the jam, curd or spread – or any filling you fancy. The world is your oyster with these tasty treats!

MAKES 20–22 COOKIES

PREP: 15 MINUTES
BAKE: 17 MINUTES

150g golden caster sugar

200g butter, softened

2 tsp vanilla bean paste

2 medium egg yolks

300g plain flour

¼ tsp sea salt

Jams, curds or spreads of your choice (about ½ tsp per cookie)

Icing sugar, for dusting

1 Beat the sugar, butter and vanilla together until pale and fluffy. Add the egg yolks and mix until combined, then beat in the flour and salt.

2 Turn out onto a work surface and form a dough, then roll into walnut-sized balls. Use your thumb to make an indentation into each ball to create the well for your chosen filling.

3 Preheat the air fryer to 160°C. Bake for 8–12 minutes. You may not need parchment paper subject to your air fryer accessories. The balls are quite solid, so they can go directly onto non-stick aeriated trays or baskets. However, if you have put the balls on parchment paper, once the cookies are almost cooked, whip the paper out from underneath them to allow the bottoms to crisp up.

4 Take the balls out of the air fryer and fill the wells with your chosen filling(s). Return to the air fryer for a further 5 minutes. Cool for 5 minutes and dust with icing sugar just before serving.

Adaptation

(DF) *Substitute the butter for vegan block butter and use jam rather than curd.*

PARMESAN AND THYME BISCUITS

These rich, moreish biscuits are epic! They are lovely served after dinner as they are essentially a cracker and cheese in one. Scale up as needed if making these for a crowd, or make little bite-sized biscuits as canapés for a drinks-and-nibbles party. If you're veggie, swap to a veggie Italian hard cheese – they do an amazing one in Paxton & Whitfield, a fantastic cheesemonger in London, and you can order online as a special treat.

**MAKES 30
BISCUITS**

PREP: 20 MINUTES

CHILL: 30 MINUTES

BAKE: 20 MINUTES

200g unsalted butter, at room temperature

60g extra virgin olive oil

2 tsp finely chopped fresh thyme

2 tsp coarse sea salt

350g plain flour, sifted, plus extra for dusting

95g Parmesan, finely grated

TIP

You can use fresh rosemary instead of thyme, if you prefer.

1 Line a baking tray with parchment paper, or use a silicone liner.

2 In a stand mixer fitted with the paddle attachment, beat the butter on low for 1–2 minutes until smooth, or beat by hand with a wooden spoon. Add the oil, thyme and salt and beat for a further 1–2 minutes until combined. Scrape down the side of the bowl and beat again on high until fluffy.

3 Add the flour and 70g of the Parmesan, and mix on low until the dough begins to come together. Beat for a further minute.

4 Shape the dough into a ball, then wrap and chill for at least 30 minutes (or overnight if you like).

5 Lightly dust a work surface with flour. Roll out the dough to about 6–7cm (2in) thick and cut into rounds using a 6cm (2in) cutter.

6 Preheat the air fryer to 170°C. Place the biscuits onto the prepared tray or in the air fryer baskets. Sprinkle with the remaining Parmesan. Bake for 16–20 minutes until firm and crisp and the edges are a deep golden.

CAKES, TRAYBAKES, MUFFINS & CUPCAKES

CLASSIC SCONES

Afternoon tea is my absolute favourite pastime! It's always such a delight to sit down to a table laden with sandwiches and treats, and of course, no afternoon tea is complete without the mighty scone! I've always had a soft spot for Cornwall as I've been going there on family holidays ever since I was a child, so for me it's always the Cornish way of serving: jam first and clotted cream on top! Whichever way you serve yours, I know you'll love the light texture of these scones.

MAKES 8–10 SCONES

PREP: 15 MINUTES

BAKE: 15 MINUTES

230g self-raising flour, plus extra for dusting

½ tsp baking powder

Pinch of sea salt

60g butter, chilled, and cut into small cubes

30g golden caster sugar

Zest of 1 lemon

150g whole milk

1 egg, beaten, to glaze

To serve

Clotted cream

Jam of your choice

1   Line a baking tray or basket with parchment paper.

2   Put the flour, baking powder and salt in a large bowl, then rub in the butter using your fingertips until the mixture resembles fine crumbs. Alternatively, blitz in a food processor and tip into a large bowl.

3   Stir in the sugar and lemon zest. Make a well in the centre of the mixture, then pour in the milk. Use a knife to bring the dough together.

4   Tip out onto a clean work surface and bring together with your hands. Gently roll out to a 3cm (1¼in) thickness on a floured work surface, making sure you don't overwork the dough. Stamp out scones using a 6cm (2in) fluted cutter. Reroll the scraps and stamp again until all the dough has been used.

5   Put the scones onto the prepared baking tray and brush with egg wash (or egg wash once they are in the basket).

6   Preheat the air fryer to 160°C. Bake for 12 minutes. Remove the parchment paper and allow the scones to crisp up for a few more minutes until risen, golden and cooked through. Check the bottoms are cooked – turn them over and bake for a further minute if the bottoms need crisping up.

7   Cool on a wire rack and serve slightly warm or at room temperature with clotted cream and jam. If freezing, freeze when cool. Defrost as needed and pop back in the air fryer on 140°C for about 2 minutes to refresh.

Adaptations

(DF) *Substitute the butter for vegan block butter. Also, substitute the clotted cream for dairy-free plant-based cream and the whole milk for plant-based milk.*

CHERRY AND ALMOND CAKE

This is my good friend Christine Lee's favourite cake. She's almond obsessed and used to eat marzipan straight out of the packet when I worked with her in my first baking job! Cherries and almonds go hand in hand, and the lemon zest gives this cake an added 'zing'.

MAKES 23CM (9IN) SQUARE CAKE (SERVES 12)
PREP: 15 MINUTES
BAKE: 45 MINUTES

175g unsalted butter, at room temperature, plus extra for greasing

150g golden caster sugar

3 medium eggs

125g self-raising flour

Zest of 1 lemon

75g ground almonds

½ tsp baking powder

Pinch of sea salt

300g fresh or canned cherries, pitted, patted dry and tossed lightly in flour

50g flaked almonds

Icing sugar, for dusting

Extra fresh cherries, to decorate

1 Grease and line a 23cm (9in) square cake tin with parchment paper.

2 In a large bowl, beat the butter and sugar for 3–5 minutes until pale and fluffy. Add the eggs one at a time, beating well after each addition, then stir through the flour, lemon zest, ground almonds, baking powder and salt.

3 Stir the flour-coated cherries through the mix, then transfer the batter to the prepared tin and poke in the remaining cherries, making sure they're just covered by the cake mixture. Scatter over the flaked almonds, making sure to press them in well so that they do not fly around in the air fryer. If you have a particularly blowy one, cover the tin with foil for the first 5 minutes of the bake.

4 Preheat the air fryer to 150°C. Bake for 40–45 minutes, or until risen and turning a dark golden colour. A skewer inserted into the centre of the cake should come out clean. Leave to cool in the tin for 10 minutes, then turn out onto a wire rack to cool completely. Dust with icing sugar and decorate with fresh cherries.

Adaptations

(DF) Substitute the butter for vegan block butter or spread.

(GF) Substitute the flour for a gluten-free blend.

TIP
These work well as cupcakes, too. Add about 75g batter to each cupcake case and bake for 20–25 minutes. It'll make around 12–14 cupcakes. Make sure the bottoms are cooked as this is quite a wet mixture, so you may wish to bake them upside-down for the last few minutes of the bake.

CHOCOLATE PEANUT BUTTER CAKE

I love this combo so much . . . almost as much as peanut butter and Marmite – don't judge me! We lived in the States for a while and we used to love those Reeses Pieces, so good! If you're a fan of peanut butter combos, make my Classic Victoria Sponge (see p84) and add some jam. Then use the buttercream from this recipe for the ultimate PB&J sponge cake!

MAKES 20CM (8IN) 3-LAYER ROUND CAKE (SERVES 14–16)
PREP: 45 MINUTES
BAKE: 18 MINUTES

For the sponge

235g unsalted butter, softened, plus extra for greasing

265g light muscovado sugar

2 tsp vanilla bean paste

4 medium eggs

225g plain chocolate, melted and cooled

170g soured cream, at room temperature

200g self-raising flour

40g cocoa powder

For the buttercream

320g smooth peanut butter (creamy style works best)

320g unsalted butter, softened

2 tsp vanilla extract or bean paste

800g icing sugar (unrefined icing sugar will taste even better as it has a caramel flavour)

50–75g whole milk, at room temperature

1 Grease and line three 20cm (8in) round cake tins, or use silicone moulds.

2 Start by making the sponge. In a stand mixer fitted with a paddle beater attachment, beat the butter, sugar and vanilla on a medium speed until pale and fluffy, or cream by hand with a wooden spoon. Reduce the speed to low and add the eggs one at a time, beating well after each addition and occasionally scraping down the side of the bowl. Pour in the melted chocolate and mix, then add the soured cream, mixing on low until incorporated.

3 In a separate bowl, mix the flour and cocoa powder together. Add this to the mixing bowl in three batches and mix on low until just incorporated. Divide the batter between the tins and level off the surfaces with a spoon.

4 Preheat the air fryer to 150°C. Bake for 15–18 minutes. A skewer inserted into the centre of the cake should come out a little fudgy. The secret to a really good chocolate cake is to slightly underbake it. Leave to cool completely in the tins on a wire rack.

5 To make the buttercream, beat the peanut butter, butter and vanilla together until really creamy on medium speed. Add the icing sugar in three batches and mix on slow until the sugar is incorporated, then increase the speed to high and beat until fluffy with each addition of the icing sugar. The mixture will be a little stiff, so add about 2 tablespoons of the milk at a time and mix on slow to loosen the buttercream. Add enough milk until you have a buttercream the consistency of soft peanut butter and feels easy to spread.

recipe continued overleaf . . .

For the chocolate drip and nut decoration

100g double cream

150g plain chocolate chips

25g golden syrup

Handful of nuts, toasted and chopped (peanuts or hazelnuts are best)

TIP

If making cupcakes, halve the ingredients used for the chocolate drip.

6   Remove the cakes from the tins and level the tops, if necessary, using a bread knife. Fill the cake with about one-third of the buttercream. If you want a very neat looking cake, it will need to be crumb coated first, followed by a second coat of buttercream (see p23). Otherwise, just spread a thick coat of buttercream straight over once filled, use a knife or spoon to make luscious flicky swirls over the cake and leave out the drip part.

7   To make the chocolate drip, melt the cream and chocolate together in a microwave-safe bowl for 1 minute at a time on medium heat until the chocolate is melted and the mixture is completely amalgamated, or do this in a bain-marie. Stir in the golden syrup. Allow to cool to room temperature until still runny but not set, and not too hot that the buttercream will melt. Pour the chocolate sauce on top, towards the centre of the cake, allowing it to pool just until the edges. Using the back of a metal spoon or palette knife, gently tease the sauce just over the edge to allow it to drip over the sides. Once you're happy with it, add a scattering of nuts.

Adaptation

GF *Substitute the flour for a gluten-free blend.*

LEMON DRIZZLE CAKE

Zesty and tangy lemon heaven in every slice. No baker's arsenal is complete without this classic bake, and now you can do it in the air fryer. Remove any guilt by telling yourself it's a palate cleanser.

MAKES 20CM (8IN) 2-LAYER ROUND CAKE (SERVES 12–14)
PREP: 20 MINUTES
BAKE: 25 MINUTES

For the sponge

200g butter, softened, plus extra for greasing

200g golden caster sugar

Zest of 1 lemon

4 medium eggs

200g self-raising flour

½ tsp baking powder

For the syrup

Juice of 1 lemon

2 tbsp icing sugar

1 tbsp boiling water

For the buttercream

125g unsalted butter, softened

1 tsp vanilla extract or bean paste

250g icing sugar

2 tbsp lemon curd

To decorate

Zest of 1 lemon or edible flowers (optional)

1   Grease and line two 20cm (8in) round cake tins, or use silicone moulds.

2   Start by making the sponge. Using a stand mixer or electric hand mixer, cream the butter, sugar and lemon zest until very pale, soft and fluffy, and the sugar granules have dissolved, or cream by hand with a wooden spoon. Add the eggs one at a time, beating well after each addition.

3   Mix the baking powder through the flour. Gradually add to the wet ingredients, one-quarter at a time, mixing gently on a low speed, until it has mostly been incorporated (fold with a metal spoon if doing this by hand). Take care not to beat too vigorously or overmix or the sponge will turn out a bit tough. Divide the batter equally between the tins.

4   Preheat the air fryer to 150°C. Bake for 20–25 minutes until a skewer inserted into the centre comes out clean.

5   While the cakes are baking, make the syrup. Mix all the ingredients together in bowl and set aside.

6   Leave the cakes in their tins for 5 minutes, then turn out onto a wire rack to cool completely and stab several times with a skewer before spooning over the syrup.

7   To make the buttercream, beat the butter until pale and soft, then mix in the vanilla. Add one-quarter of the icing sugar and slowly mix until incorporated, then increase the speed. Repeat to use up all the icing sugar (you can add a splash of just-boiled water to help with the texture and to make the buttercream whiter).

8   Spread one of the cakes with the lemon curd, then smooth over the buttercream (pipe the buttercream if you want a fancy finish), then sandwich with the second sponge. If there is any syrup left over, drizzle it over the top and decorate with lemon zest or edible flowers, if using.

PINA COLADA CUPCAKES

These cupcakes are the perfect bake for summer, or to bring on summer vibes whatever the time of year. They are ideal for parties . . . a cake and cocktail in one, and they look so pretty, too! Add a bit of kitsch styling to your bakes with a retro cocktail umbrella!

MAKES 12 CUPCAKES
PREP: 20 MINUTES
BAKE: 15 MINUTES

For the sponge

435g can crushed pineapple in juice

150g coconut oil, melted, or sunflower oil

175g golden caster sugar

60g coconut cream

3 medium eggs

200g self-raising flour

1 tsp baking powder

For the syrup

60g pineapple juice (from the can)

2 tbsp caster sugar

50g Malibu or white rum

For the buttercream and decoration

250g unsalted butter, softened

500g icing sugar, sifted

60g coconut cream

60g Malibu or white rum

Fresh pineapple slices

50g coconut flakes, toasted (optional)

12 cocktail cherries

1 Line two six-hole cupcake tins with paper cases, or use individual silicone moulds.

2 Start by making the sponge. Drain the can of pineapple in a sieve and reserve the juice for the syrup.

3 In a stand mixer fitted with a paddle attachment (or by hand) beat the oil and sugar together, then whisk in the coconut cream. Add the eggs one at a time, beating well after each addition. Beat in 225g of the crushed pineapple. Fold in the flour and baking powder. Divide the batter equally between the cases.

4 Preheat the air fryer to 150°C. Bake for 12–15 minutes until deep golden brown and a skewer inserted into the centre of a cupcake comes out clean. Check that the bottoms are cooked – you may need to turn the cupcakes over and bake upside-down for a couple more minutes.

5 Meanwhile, make the syrup. Heat the reserved pineapple juice, sugar and 40g of water in a small saucepan and bring to the boil over a medium heat, stirring until the sugar has dissolved. Simmer for about 2 minutes until slightly thickened. Add the Malibu and simmer for a further minute.

6 As soon as the cupcakes are ready, remove them from the air fryer and brush the syrup generously over the tops. The liquid should soak into the sponges. Cool in the cases for 5 minutes, then transfer to a wire rack to cool completely.

7 To make the buttercream, put the butter into the stand mixer bowl (or mixing bowl) and beat on medium speed until pale and fluffy. Gradually add the icing sugar, beating well after each addition, then add the coconut cream, beating until light and fluffy. Add the Malibu and beat again.

8 To decorate, transfer the buttercream to a piping bag fitted with a large star nozzle (1M) and pipe tall swirls over the cupcakes. Top with a wedge of pineapple, sprinkle over some coconut flakes, if using, and top with a cocktail cherry.

TIP
If you're short
of time, use shop-
bought vanilla or
lemon buttercream
and mix in a dash
of rum.

BRUCE CHOCOLATE FUDGE CAKE

This gorgeous fudge cake is based on the cake I made for the recent Matilda movie. It's named after the character that devours it. It's really easy to mix up, and the icing is lusciously glossy, velvety and decadent. You'll see why Bruce couldn't resist it once you take a bite!

MAKES 20CM (8IN) 2-LAYER ROUND CAKE (SERVES 12–14)

PREP: 45 MINUTES
CHILL: 20 MINUTES
BAKE: 22 MINUTES

For the sponge

75g cocoa powder

125g boiling water

275g golden caster sugar

160g sunflower oil, plus extra for greasing

2 medium eggs

2 tsp vanilla extract

150g whole milk

225g self-raising flour, sifted

1 tsp baking powder

½ tsp fine sea salt

For the icing

400g dark chocolate, chopped into small pieces, or chocolate chips

280g double cream

150g icing sugar, sieved

120g butter, softened

¼ tsp sea salt

To decorate

9 cocktail cherries with stems on for dressing (optional)

1   Grease and line two 20cm (8in) round cake tins, or use silicone moulds.

2   Start by making the sponge. Whisk the cocoa powder and boiling water together until smooth.

3   Put the sugar in a large bowl, pour over the oil and whisk until combined and lump free. Beat in the eggs. Mix in the cocoa mixture, along with the vanilla and milk. Add the flour, baking powder and salt, and whisk until smooth, then divide equally between the tins.

4   Preheat the air fryer to 150°C. Bake for 18–22 minutes until well risen and a skewer inserted into the centre comes out almost clean. Leave to cool in the tins for a few minutes, then turn out onto a wire rack to cool completely.

5   To make the icing, put the chocolate in a bowl. Boil the cream and pour it over the chocolate, placing a plate on top of the bowl to trap the heat. Leave for 5 minutes, then mix with a wooden spoon, stirring in one direction until the ganache comes together. If there are any lumps of chocolate you can gently heat again until completely melted in the bowl set over simmering water. Set aside to cool for about 30 minutes at room temperature, but do not allow to set.

6   Whisk in the icing sugar with an electric hand whisk or balloon whisk until really smooth. Then whisk in the butter until you have a glossy, whippy icing. It should feel soft enough to spread over the cake but still hold its shape. If it needs to cool down a little to firm up, leave it; you just need to stir it every now and again to make sure it doesn't harden. (If it does set a little, pop it in the microwave for 5–10 seconds to soften up and whisk again to make sure it's smooth.)

recipe continued overleaf . . .

7   Trim the top of one cake to level, if needed. Place it on a plate or stand, trimmed-side up, and spread a generous amount of icing over the cake. Sandwich with the second cake, inverting it so that the flat side that was the bottom is uppermost. Line up and gently press together, running a palette knife around the edge to smooth over and fill the gap between the layers. Refrigerate for 20 minutes or freeze for 10 minutes.

8   To finish, put the remaining icing in one heap on the top of the cake, then use a palette knife to spread it over the top and sides – having a turntable is useful. Spin the cake around, using the end of a small palette knife to do the swirl around the edge in lines going up around the sides, then on the top swirling from the outside inwards. If you don't have a turntable and palette knife, just use a regular knife and make luscious flicks in the icing for texture. Decorate with cherries, if you wish. Prepare to fight off the Trunchbull!

9   The cake will keep for up to 5 days if stored in an airtight container, or can be frozen for up to a month.

Adaptations

(DF) *Substitute the butter for vegan block butter, ensure chocolate is dairy-free, use plant-based milk and use dairy-free cream in the icing.*

(GF) *Substitute the flour for a gluten-free blend.*

BANANA, PECAN AND CARAMEL BREAD

This is next-level banana bread with added caramel and nuts. Texture-wise, it's a cross between banana bread and cake. It's so quick to make and it's great for using up overripe bananas. I peel any overripe bananas and freeze them – nothing gets wasted in my house if I can help it (apart from me, occasionally!).

**MAKES 450G
(1LB) LOAF**
PREP: 30 MINUTES
BAKE: 55 MINUTES

For the sponge

100g butter at room temperature, plus extra for greasing

50g golden caster sugar

40g light muscovado sugar

1 tsp vanilla extract or bean paste

1 small, very ripe banana (75–100g peeled weight), cut into small chunks

40g ground almonds

2 medium eggs

50g whole milk

80g self-raising flour

1 tsp baking powder

60g pecans, finely chopped

For the topping (optional)

2 tbsp store-bought caramel or toffee sauce

Handful of whole pecans

Handful of banana chips

1   Grease and line a 450g (1lb) loaf tin with parchment paper.

2   Start by making the sponge. Beat the butter, both sugars and vanilla until pale and fluffy on medium speed for about 2 minutes. Add the banana and beat on slow to combine, then beat in the ground almonds.

3   Add the eggs one at a time, beating well after each addition. Scrape down the side of the bowl as needed. Add the milk, flour and baking powder and mix on slow until you have a smooth batter, then mix in the pecans.

4   Preheat the air fryer to 150°C. Pour the batter into the prepared tin. Bake for 45–55 minutes until golden and risen, and a skewer inserted into the centre comes out clean. Cool in the tin for 10 minutes, then lift out. Slice and serve, or to decorate, drizzle over some caramel sauce and stud with more pecans and banana chips.

5   Keeps for up to 3 days or can be frozen for up to 3 months.

Adaptations

(DF) *Substitute the butter for vegan block butter or spread and the whole milk for plant-based milk.*

(GF) *Substitute the flour for a gluten-free blend.*

> **TIP**
> *If you'd rather make mini loaves, use individual mini loaf tins instead and bake for about 15 minutes.*

BISCOFF BROWNIES

This is my 'mothership' brownie recipe. I developed this recipe when there was an egg shortage. I've used Biscoff biscuits and spread because they are a favourite in our household, but you can swap the biscuits for any kind and replace the swirl for another spread, such as Nutella, hazelnut cream or your favourite nut butter. To keep this recipe plant-based, make sure none of the ingredients you're subbing in include any milk.

MAKES 20–23CM (8–9IN) BROWNIE
PREP: 20 MINUTES
BAKE: 35 MINUTES

100g vegan spread (or any butter you prefer)

250g dark chocolate, chopped, or chocolate chips

125g golden caster sugar

125g light muscovado sugar

300g oat milk (or any milk you prefer)

2 tsp vanilla extract or bean paste

185g plain flour

30g cocoa powder

½ tsp sea salt

190g Biscoff biscuits

250g Biscoff spread

130g Biscoff cream biscuits

1   Line a baking tin or the air fryer basket (if it's a similar size) with parchment paper.

2   In a large mixing bowl, melt the butter, chocolate and both sugars in the microwave in 30-second bursts, stirring between bursts until combined (or you can do this in a saucepan on a very low heat). Don't let the mixture get too hot – you want the chocolate to melt but not be hot. Gradually whisk in the milk and vanilla.

3   In a separate large bowl, whisk the flour, cocoa powder and salt together, then fold into the wet mixture.

4   Preheat the air fryer to 150°C. Line the paper lined basket or tin with 140g of the Biscoff biscuits to cover the bottom. Pour the batter into the tin or basket.

5   Melt the Biscoff spread in the microwave for 20 seconds or stand the jar in hot water to melt, then spoon blobs of it into the batter and drag with a knife to create a marble effect. Break up the remaining 50g of Biscoff biscuits and plunge them into the mixture, scattering some crumbles on top. Decorate with the Biscoff cream biscuits.

6   Bake for 30–35 minutes (depending on the size of your tin or basket). The brownie should be set around the edges but slightly underbaked and fudgy in the middle. A skewer inserted into the centre should come out with a paste-like texture – not glistening, but not dry – and it should have a nice wobble. Remember, it will set more firmly as it cools. You can put this in the fridge once cool so it will be easier to cut – the texture goes really gooey, almost like a chocolate truffle. Cut into squares and serve.

7   Well wrapped, it will keep for 5–7 days, and it can also be frozen.

Adaptation

GF Substitute the flour for a gluten-free blend and make sure any biscuits, spreads and milks are gluten-free too.

BLUEBERRY LEMON CAKE

This delicate lemon and blueberry sponge is light in texture and a breeze to make. I've added a quick luscious buttercream dotted with jam to add flavour and colour. Using a toothed scraper is a fab fast way to elevate your cakes, as the texture and colour will hide any imperfections, so you don't have to worry about being super-neat with this cake. Make sure all the ingredients are room temperature.

MAKES 15CM (6IN) 2-LAYER ROUND CAKE (SERVES 8–10)

PREP: 45 MINUTES

BAKE: 30 MINUTES

For the sponge

135g softened butter, plus extra for greasing

100g full-fat Greek yoghurt, plus extra to serve

3 medium eggs

Zest and juice of 1 lemon, plus extra zest to decorate

150g self-raising flour

135g golden caster sugar

150g blueberries, plus extra to serve

For the buttercream

250g unsalted butter, softened

500g icing sugar, sifted

1 tsp vanilla extract

A little milk, to loosen

3 tbsp blueberry jam

1 Grease and line two 15cm (6in) round cake tins, or use silicone moulds.

2 Start by making the sponge. Put the butter, yoghurt, eggs, lemon zest and juice, flour and sugar in a large bowl. Mix briefly with an electric whisk until the batter just comes together. Divide half the batter equally between the prepared tins. Sprinkle over half the blueberries, then top with the remaining batter. Sprinkle over the remaining blueberries.

3 Preheat the air fryer to 140°C. Bake for 25–30 minutes until risen, golden and slightly shrinking away from the sides. A skewer inserted into the centre should come out clean.

4 Cool in the tins for 10–15 minutes, then turn out onto a wire rack to cool completely. Trim the tops of the cakes to level them, if needed.

5 To make the buttercream, beat the butter until smooth and creamy, then gradually beat in the icing sugar and vanilla until you have a light, smooth and fluffy buttercream. Loosen with a little milk to make it easier to spread but make sure it still holds its shape.

6 Place one cake onto a plate or stand and spread over about 150g of buttercream. Make a well in the middle with a palette knife, pushing the buttercream out to the edge, and fill the middle with 2 tablespoons of the jam. Place the second cake on top and cover the top and sides of both cakes with the remaining buttercream, using a palette knife to spread it around.

7 Using the tip of a knife or the back of a teaspoon, splodge dots of the remaining jam around the sides and dot over the top, then using a toothed scraper, drag around the outside to sweep the jam through. Use the tip of a palette knife or the handle of a teaspoon to make a circular swirl over the top of the cake to add a spiral design and sweep the jam through the icing.

TIP
The quantities
shown here will
make 6–8 cupcakes.
Bake for 18–20
minutes.

TIPS

• Multiply the quantities by 1.5 if you'd rather make a 20cm (8in) 2-layer round coffee and walnut cake. Bake for 22–25 minutes.

• Toast walnuts in the air fryer at 150°C. Use a small dish covered in foil so that the nuts don't get blown about!

COFFEE AND WALNUT SQUARES

This recipe makes dainty little toasted walnut and coffee cake cubes – afternoon tea wouldn't be the same without them!

MAKES 9 SQUARES
PREP: 45 MINUTES
BAKE: 25 MINUTES

For the sponge

150g unsalted butter, softened, plus extra for greasing

75g golden caster sugar

75g light muscovado sugar

1 tsp vanilla extract

3 medium eggs

3 tsp strong espresso powder mixed with a little boiled water

130g self-raising flour

½ tsp baking powder

¼ tsp fine sea salt

85g walnuts, chopped

For the buttercream

150g walnuts, toasted

140g unsalted butter, softened

40g cream cheese

1 tsp vanilla extract

275g icing sugar

2 tsp strong espresso powder mixed with a little boiled water

1　Grease and line an 18cm (7in) square cake tin, or use a silicone mould.

2　Start by making the sponge. Cream the butter and both sugars together until pale and fluffy. Add the vanilla and the eggs one at a time, beating well after each addition and scraping down the bowl as needed. Add the coffee paste and mix on a low speed.

3　In a separate bowl, mix the flour, baking powder and salt together. Add the flour into the wet mixture and mix until incorporated, being careful not to overmix as it will make the sponge tough. Stir in the walnuts and pour into the prepared tin, levelling the surface.

4　Preheat the air fryer to 150°C. Bake the sponge for 20–25 minutes until springy and a skewer inserted into the centre comes out clean. Leave to cool in the tin for 10 minutes, then turn out onto a wire rack to cool completely.

5　Blitz the cooled toasted walnuts in a food processor, or chop very finely.

6　To make the buttercream, beat the butter, cream cheese and vanilla together until soft and creamy, then add one-third of the icing sugar at a time, mixing slowly until well incorporated, then increase the speed and whisk until light and fluffy. Mix in the coffee.

7　Trim the top of the cake to level it, then cut it into 9 equal squares. Spread the sides of each square with a thin coating of buttercream and press some chopped walnuts into the sides. Use a cake smoother if you have one to help press them against the coating so you don't have fingerprint marks, or use the flat of your palm.

8　To finish, add the remaining buttercream to a piping bag fitted with a petal nozzle (I use Wilton 104) and pipe ruffles over the top of each square. The squares will keep for 3 days in an airtight container in the fridge, or can be frozen. Bring them to room temperature before serving.

RED VELVET CUPCAKES

Red velvet cakes are absolutely iconic; I love how they look. The dreamy cream cheese topping on the light vanilla cocoa sponge is a winner. These cakes were one of the most popular in my bakery, Fancy Nancy. We made thousands of these, and they would always sell out! This recipe works both as cupcakes or as a layer cake.

MAKES 12 CUPCAKES

PREP: 30 MINUTES

BAKE: 25 MINUTES

For the sponge

190g salted butter, softened

165g golden caster sugar

2 medium eggs

20g cocoa powder

2 tsp vanilla extract

2 tsp strong red food colouring gel (I used Sugarflair Red Extra)

225g self-raising flour

½ tsp sea salt

175g buttermilk

1 tsp white vinegar or apple cider vinegar

1 tsp bicarbonate of soda

For the icing

250g unsalted butter, softened

150g full-fat cream cheese, at room temperature

2 tsp vanilla bean paste

500g icing sugar

1   Line two six-hole cupcake tins with paper cases, or use individual silicone moulds.

2   Start by making the sponge. Put the butter and sugar in the bowl of a stand mixer fitted with the beater attachment and cream for 2–3 minutes on medium speed until pale, light and fluffy, or cream by hand with a wooden spoon. Add the eggs one at a time, beating well after each addition.

3   In a small bowl, mix together the cocoa powder, vanilla extract and red food colouring with about 2 tablespoons of hot water to form a paste. Add this to the cake mixture and mix well until combined.

4   In a separate bowl, mix the flour and salt together.

5   Add one-third of the buttermilk to the batter mixture, then add one-third of the flour. Alternate adding the buttermilk and flour until everything is fully combined, taking care not to overmix.

6   In a small bowl, mix together the vinegar and bicarbonate of soda and add this to the cake mixture. Beat until smooth. Divide the batter equally between the cupcake cases, filling them about three-quarters full as they do shrink after they have risen.

7   Preheat the air fryer to 150°C. Bake for 22–25 minutes until springy to the touch and a skewer inserted into the centres comes out clean. Don't open the air fryer for at least 20 minutes or the cakes may sink!

8   After this time, remove the cakes from the air fryer and leave to cool in their tins for 10 minutes, then turn them out onto a wire rack to cool completely. Take care as they are very delicate.

recipe continued overleaf . . .

9   To make the icing, put the butter, cream cheese and vanilla in the bowl of a stand mixer fitted with the beater attachment. Beat on high speed for about 1 minute until the mixture is very creamy and smooth. Gradually add the icing sugar, about one-quarter at a time, beating after each addition, slowly at first to just incorporate, then on high speed for about 1 minute.

10 Fill a piping bag fitted with a large round nozzle (I use Wilton 2a), or cut a hole in a food bag, and pipe the icing onto the cupcakes. If you like the idea of a red crumb topping, you will have to sacrifice one cupcake to crumble over the others, or you can trim a little off of the top of each cake and crumble, if you prefer. It does look very pretty!

TIP

To make a 2-layer cake, double the quantity of ingredients and grease and line two 20cm (8in) round tins, or use silicone moulds. Bake for 25–28 minutes, and don't open the door until 20 minutes have elapsed.

BANANA AND CHOCOLATE MUFFINS

Chocolate and banana make such a great combo – everyone will love these muffins. This recipe is completely flexible: you can use dairy or plant milk, and use a regular egg or substitute for a flax egg – either way, these muffins will taste amazing! It's always handy to have some recipes up your sleeve that will suit everyone, including those with allergies, so this one is a winner.

MAKES 5-6 MUFFINS

PREP: 10 MINUTES
BAKE: 14 MINUTES

---

1 medium ripe banana (about 100g peeled weight)

1 tbsp olive oil (or any oil you like)

80g tahini (well stirred)

2 tbsp milk

1 medium egg

50g light muscovado or soft light brown sugar

¼ tsp fine sea salt

25g cocoa powder, sifted

60g ground almonds

40g oats

1 tsp baking powder

30g dark chocolate chips, plus extra for sprinkling

TIP
To make this recipe plant based, replace the egg with flax egg by mixing 1 tablespoon of ground flax with 40g of water. This is a good binder in plant-based recipes.

1 Line a six-hole muffin tin with paper cases, or use individual silicone moulds.

2 Put the banana into a food processor with the oil, tahini, milk and egg, then blitz until smooth. Alternatively, you can use a stick blender or mash well by hand in a bowl.

3 Add the sugar, salt and cocoa powder and pulse to combine. Use a spatula to scrape down the side of the food processor, then add the ground almonds, oats and baking powder and blitz a few times to combine. Add the chocolate chips and pulse a couple more times.

4 Divide the batter equally between the cases, filling almost all the way to the top. Sprinkle on a few more chocolate chips.

5 Preheat the air fryer to 160°C. Bake for 12–14 minutes. The muffins are ready when a skewer inserted into the centre comes out almost clean, with a little fudgy paste on it, but not glistening wet.

6 Leave the muffins to cool in their cases for about 5 minutes, then transfer to a wire rack. These are lovely served a little warm or at room temperature. They keep for 3 days or can be frozen for up to a month (defrost at room temperature before serving).

Adaptations

(DF) *Use plant milk and dairy-free chocolate.*

(GF) *Make sure the oats are gluten free.*

(PB) *Make the dairy-free substitutions above. Substitute the egg for flax egg (see Tip).*

CLASSIC VICTORIA SPONGE

Another simple staple that works really well in the air fryer. Some like it sandwiched with buttercream, others with cream – there's no right or wrong, it's up to you! The benefit of using buttercream is you don't have to refrigerate it.

MAKES 20CM (8IN) 2-LAYER ROUND CAKE (SERVES 12–14)

PREP: 30 MINUTES
BAKE: 22 MINUTES

For the sponge

200g unsalted butter, very soft, plus extra for greasing

200g caster sugar

½ tsp vanilla extract or bean paste

4 medium eggs

200g self-raising flour

1 tsp baking powder

½ tsp sea salt

For the buttercream

125g unsalted butter, softened

½ tsp vanilla extract or bean paste

220g icing sugar, sifted, plus extra for dusting

2–3 tbsp raspberry or strawberry jam

For a cream filling

If you prefer a cream filling to buttercream, whip 300g of double cream with 1 tablespoon of caster sugar or icing sugar and ½ teaspoon of vanilla extract to soft peaks.

---

1   Grease and line two 20cm (8in) round cake tins, or use silicone moulds.

2   Start by making the sponge. Put the butter, sugar and vanilla in a bowl/stand mixer and beat on high (or if you're using a wooden spoon, use plenty of elbow grease!). Add the eggs one at a time, beating well after each addition.

3   In a separate bowl, mix together the flour, baking powder and salt. Add to the wet mixture one-quarter at a time, mixing gently on a low speed, until it has mostly been incorporated, or fold with a metal spoon or spatula if doing by hand. Take care not to mix too vigorously or the sponge can turn out a bit tough. Divide the batter into the prepared tins.

4   Preheat the air fryer to 150°C. Bake for 18–22 minutes. Leave to cool in the tins for about 5 minutes, then turn out onto a wire rack to cool completely.

5   To make the buttercream, beat the butter until pale and soft, then mix in the vanilla. Add one-quarter of the icing sugar and slowly mix until incorporated. Then increase the speed and beat well. Repeat until all the icing sugar has been incorporated.

6   Level the top of one cake using a bread knife, then spread the jam on top. If you want to make the cake look a bit fancy, transfer the buttercream into a piping bag and pipe the filling, or simply spread with a palette knife or the back of a spoon. Sandwich with the second cake on top. Dust generously with icing sugar.

7   The cake will keep for up to 3 days. The sponges freeze well for up to a month without the filling.

Adaptations

(DF) *Substitute the butter for vegan block butter and the cream for a whippable dairy-free plant-based cream.*

(GF) *Substitute the flour for a gluten-free blend.*

TIP
Add a splash of just-boiled water to the buttercream to help with the texture and to make it whiter.

CHOCOLATE AND BEETROOT CAKE

This chocolate and beetroot cake is a classic flavour combination. Whoever first put these two ingredients together was a genius! It has a deep chocolate flavour that's really complemented by the earthy beetroot. Serve with tangy crème fraîche.

MAKES 20CM (8IN) ROUND CAKE (SERVES 8–10)

PREP: 20 MINUTES
COOL: 30 MINUTES
BAKE: 35 MINUTES

For the sponge

80g dark chocolate, finely chopped

115g self-raising flour

20g cocoa powder

1 tsp baking powder

¼ tsp sea salt

160g cooked beetroot

125g light muscovado sugar

2 medium eggs

125g sunflower oil, plus extra for greasing

For the ganache

140g double cream

160g dark chocolate

50g golden syrup

1   Grease and line an 20cm (8in) round cake tin, or use a silicone mould.

2   Start by making the sponge. Melt the chocolate in a microwave-safe bowl in 30-second bursts, or melt in a bain-marie. Set aside to cool.

3   In a large bowl, mix the flour, cocoa powder, baking powder and salt.

4   In a food processor, blend the beetroot until very smooth, scraping down the side of the bowl if necessary to ensure it is fully blended. Add the sugar and blend again until smooth. Add the eggs one at a time, beating well after each addition, then pour in the oil. Blend until smooth, then add the cooled melted chocolate and briefly blend to mix through. Stir the wet mixture into the dry mixture and pour into the prepared tin.

5   Preheat the air fryer to 150°C. Bake for 30–35 minutes, or until a skewer inserted into the centre comes out almost clean but still a little fudgy. Leave to cool for 10 minutes, then turn out of the tin and leave to cool completely on a wire rack.

6   To make the ganache, gently melt all the ingredients together in a non-stick pan until thick, lump free and glistening. Leave to cool for about 30 minutes to a spreadable consistency.

7   Spoon the ganache on top of the cake, spread out to the edges and make a swirl with a palette knife or spoon. Leave to set, then slice and serve with a dollop of crème fraîche.

Adaptations

(DF) *Substitute the cream for dairy-free plant-based cream and use dairy-free chocolate.*

(GF) *Substitute the flour for a gluten-free blend.*

Fast forward

If you're short of time, top the cake with Nutella or chocolate spread, or simply dust with icing sugar.

PISTACHIO AND RICOTTA CAKE

Ricotta and olive oil replace the butter in this cake, and yoghurt replaces buttercream for the topping, so this bake is lower in saturated fat but still lovely and moist. Plus, all those nuts and berries make this so delicious – an ideal choice for a dessert and a much healthier option, too.

MAKES 20CM (8IN) ROUND CAKE (SERVES 10–12)
PREP: 30 MINUTES
BAKE: 30 MINUTES

For the sponge

150g shelled pistachios (or a mix of these and ground almonds, or all ground almonds)

115g self-raising flour

1 tsp baking powder

185g caster sugar

3 medium eggs

180g ricotta cheese

75g light olive oil, plus extra for greasing

Zest and juice of 1 orange

For the topping

150g plain or vanilla yoghurt

A little honey or maple syrup (optional)

150g mixed berries or sliced fruits

A few fresh mint leaves (optional)

1 Grease and line a 20cm (8in) round cake tin.

2 Start by making the sponge. Blitz the pistachios in a food processor until coarsely ground, or use ground almonds if you do not have a food processor. Sift the flour and baking powder into the bowl with the nuts.

3 In a separate bowl, whisk the sugar and eggs for about 5 minutes until pale and thick using a stand mixer or an electric whisk, or by hand. Add the ricotta, oil, orange zest and juice, and mix gently until just combined. Fold in the nutty flour, then pour into the prepared tin and level off the top with a spoon.

4 Preheat the air fryer to 160°C. Bake for 25–30 minutes, or until risen and golden and a skewer inserted into the centre comes out clean. Leave to cool in the tin for 20 minutes, then carefully turn out onto a wire rack to cool completely.

5 To make the topping, sweeten the yoghurt, if desired, with a little honey or maple syrup, then spread over the cake. Scatter over the mixed berries, or create a fruit mosaic topping with evenly cut fruit slices (use scissors to trim the fruit to get neat rounded edges). Garnish with a few fresh mint leaves, if you like.

TIPS

• Decorate with your favourite seasonal fruit. Other fruits that work well include whole blueberries, sliced strawberries, kiwis, oranges, kumquats, satsumas and blackberries.

• You can substitute some or all the pistachios for almonds.

PINEAPPLE UPSIDE-DOWN CAKE

To me, this cake is so retro and iconic, it really reminds me of my childhood. Perhaps I'll write my next book on 1970s recipes! Bring back mushroom vol-au-vents and cheese and pineapple on sticks, I say. Who's with me?!

MAKES 23CM (9IN) SQUARE CAKE (SERVES 12)

PREP: 25 MINUTES
BAKE: 50 MINUTES

For the pineapple layer

75g unsalted butter, softened, plus extra for greasing

75g caster sugar

9 canned pineapple rings, well drained

21 glacé cherries

For the sponge

200g unsalted butter, softened

200g caster sugar

1 tsp vanilla bean paste

4 medium eggs

200g self-raising flour

½ tsp baking powder, sieved into the flour

1 Grease and line a 23cm (9in) square cake tin.

2 Start by making the pineapple layer. Cream together the butter and sugar until soft and pale, then spread in an even layer over the base and up the sides of the prepared tin.

3 Arrange the pineapple rings over the base first, then place the glacé cherries in the centre of each ring and in any gaps.

4 To make the sponge, cream the butter, sugar and vanilla together for a few minutes until pale and fluffy. Add the eggs one at a time, beating well after each addition. Fold in the flour and baking powder. Carefully spoon the batter into the pineapple-lined tin and level off with a spoon.

5 Preheat the air fryer to 150°C. Bake for 45–50 minutes until the sponge is cooked through.

6 Leave to cool in the tin for 10 minutes. Place a large plate over the tin and carefully turn out the cake and remove the paper to reveal the pretty pineapple pattern. Serve either warm with ice cream or custard or at room temperature for tea time with a cuppa.

Adaptions

DF *Substitute the butter for vegan block butter or spread.*
GF *Substitute the flour for a gluten-free blend.*

CLOTTED CREAM BUNDT CAKE

Cornwall is very close to my heart as we used to go there on holiday when I was little, and of course, Cornish clotted cream is the best! Using clotted cream in place of butter makes for a gorgeously light sponge. This recipe is pretty nifty because all you need is a bowl, sieve, spoon and cake tin, as you can use the clotted cream pot for measuring out if you don't have scales, so it's a handy hack for those that have minimal kitchen equipment. I've baked mine in a 5-cup bundt tin but you can just use a 20cm (8in) round tin. If edible flowers are in season, they look lovely on this cake.

**MAKES 20CM
(8IN) ROUND CAKE
(SERVES 10–12)**
PREP: 20 MINUTES
BAKE: 40 MINUTES

Butter, for greasing

227g tub of Rodda's Cornish clotted cream

200–210g golden caster sugar (or fill the clotted cream pot to the same level as the clotted cream was)

4 medium eggs

220g self-raising flour (fill the clotted cream pot to the top)

1 tsp baking powder

Pinch of sea salt

½ tsp culinary lavender grains

Zest of 1 lemon

Icing sugar, for dusting

Sprig of lavender and edible flowers, to decorate (optional)

For the glacé icing

150g sifted icing sugar

1 tbsp lemon juice

1 Grease a bundt tin with butter and dust in a little extra flour to allow easy release or grease and line a 20cm (8in) round cake tin with parchment paper.

2 Spoon the clotted cream into a large bowl. Add the sugar and mix with a wooden spoon until smooth and creamy. Add the eggs one at a time, beating well after each addition. Sift the flour, baking powder and salt into the bowl, then fold in the lavender and lemon zest until you have a smooth batter. Pour into the prepared tin.

3 Preheat the air fryer to 150°C. Bake for 35–40 minutes until the cake is risen, golden and shrinking away from the edges a little. A skewer inserted into the centre should come out clean.

4 Leave to cool in the tin for 10 minutes, then turn out onto a wire rack to cool completely and remove the paper lining. Make a simple glacé icing with icing sugar mixed the lemon juice and a few drops of water to give a thick but runny icing and decorate with a sprig of lavender and edible flowers, if using.

Adaptation
GF *Substitute the flour for a gluten-free blend.*

TIP
You can omit the lavender altogether if it's not your thing, or replace the lavender with orange or lemon zest.

OLIVE OIL CAKE

I love this cake as the texture is so light and crumbly, thanks to the olive oil. I used orange zest and rosemary, but you can use lemon zest and thyme if you prefer. It's inspired by a famous cake called the 'Bomb Ass Cake' from a bakery which I used to visit whenever we were in LA. It has a huge reputation and this is my homage to it!

MAKES 20CM (8IN) ROUND CAKE (SERVES 10–12)

PREP: 20 MINUTES

BAKE: 55 MINUTES

---

3 medium eggs

150g golden caster sugar

95g olive oil, plus extra for greasing

Zest of 1 orange

50g juice (from the orange)

2 tsp finely chopped rosemary leaves

175g plain flour

1 tsp baking powder

½ tsp bicarbonate of soda

Icing sugar and sprigs of rosemary, to decorate

1   Grease and line a 20cm (8in) round cake tin, or use a silicone mould.

2   In a bowl, beat the eggs and sugar on medium–high speed for 2 minutes until pale, creamy and slightly thickened. Add the oil and beat well for a further minute or so. Add the orange zest, orange juice and rosemary, and beat to combine.

3   Mix the flour, baking powder and bicarbonate of soda together, then gently fold this through the wet mixture in batches. Pour the mixture into the prepared tin.

4   Preheat the air fryer to 150°C. Bake for 50–55 minutes until cooked through and springy. Check on the cake – if it is turning too dark, reduce the temperature to 140°C for the last part of the bake, or cover with foil.

5   Leave to cool in the tin for 15 minutes, then turn out onto a wire rack to cool completely.

6   For a really neat finish, place the paper back around the side of the cake and dredge some icing sugar all over the top to generously coat. Decorate with sprigs of rosemary.

CHEESE AND SPRING ONION SCONES

I first made these for my baking club during wild garlic season, which is mid-February through to April. If you love wild garlic and can get hold of it, it's gorgeous in place of the spring onions, and so pretty with a wild garlic leaf baked on the top!

MAKES 10–12 SCONES
PREP: 15 MINUTES
BAKE: 18 MINUTES

325g self-raising flour, plus extra for dusting

½ tsp baking powder

½ tsp sea salt

80g butter

225g extra-mature Cheddar, grated

75g green spring onion tops, chopped, plus a few lengths for the tops

1–2 tsp mustard powder

1 medium egg

150g milk

1 egg, beaten, to glaze

1 Sift the flour, baking powder and salt into a large mixing bowl. Rub in the butter using your fingertips until the mixture resembles fine crumbs (or use a food processor). Add the cheese, spring onions and mustard powder and mix together.

2 In a separate bowl, beat the egg and milk together and add to the dry mixture to make a soft, but not sticky dough. Knead the dough lightly, then turn it onto a floured work surface and pat gently into a ball. Use a lightly floured rolling pin to roll out the dough to about 2.5cm (1in) thick.

3 Using a 6cm (2¼in) round cutter, cut out rounds, reroll the scraps and cut again until all the dough has been used. Glaze with egg wash and add a few lengths of spring onion tops on top of each scone.

4 Preheat the air fryer to 160°C. Bake for 15–18 minutes until completely cooked and deep golden. Flip the scones over for the last 2 minutes to brown the bottoms.

5 Best eaten warm. Serve with extra butter and cheese, if liked.

CHEESE AND MARMITE MUFFINS

These utterly moreish muffins are to die for. Devour them straight from the oven if you can't wait! I've added a chunk of Marmite cheese in the centre. They work fine without, but it comes as a nice surprise!

MAKES 6 MUFFINS
PREP: 15 MINUTES
BAKE: 16 MINUTES

200g self-raising flour

1 tsp baking powder

Pinch of sea salt and freshly ground black pepper

80g strong Cheddar, grated, plus 40g for sprinkling

50g butter

1–1½ tbsp Marmite

1 medium egg

90g milk

6 small chunks of Marmite cheese, or Cheddar

1 Line a six-hole muffin tin with paper cases, or use individual silicone moulds.

2 In a large bowl, mix the flour, baking powder and seasoning together, then stir through the grated cheese.

3 In a small saucepan, melt the butter on a gentle heat and stir in the Marmite until combined.

4 Beat the egg in a bowl, then pour into the buttery Marmite mixture with the milk, and beat to combine. Pour the wet mixture onto the dry mixture and mix thoroughly.

5 Half-fill the muffin cases with the batter, drop in a chunk of cheese, then top with more batter. Sprinkle over the remaining grated Cheddar.

6 Preheat the air fryer to 160°C. Bake for 13–16 minutes. Check the muffins are cooked at the bottom – turn them upside-down for the last 1–2 minutes, if needed.

7 Allow to cool for as long as you can resist before devouring these mighty savoury morsels. Even better if enjoyed with a glass of wine!

PIES & PASTRIES

CHOCOLATE GANACHE TARTLETS

I made these tartlets for my kids as an after-dinner pudding when they were all vegan. You don't have to make them vegan, and you can use regular butter or cream if you prefer, but they are so delicious and a great recipe to have in your back pocket for those with food allergies (except peanuts of course). If you don't want to use salted peanuts because of an allergy, toasted hazelnuts make a nice swap for this recipe.

MAKES 4 TARTLETS

PREP: 30 MINUTES

BAKE: 21 MINUTES

CHILL: 30 MINUTES

For the pastry

200g plain flour, plus extra for dusting

100g vegan block butter, chilled (make sure it's a harder one for pastries, e.g. Trex, Naturli or Flora)

65g salted peanuts, blitzed or very finely chopped

2–3 tbsp cold water

For the chocolate ganache filling

200g good-quality dark dairy-free chocolate

150g dairy-free plant-based cream (Elmlea works really well)

30g golden syrup

To decorate

Fresh berries or edible flowers and gold leaf (optional)

1 Lightly grease four 10cm (4in) fluted tartlet cases.

2 Start by making the pastry. In a food processor, blitz together the flour and butter until the mixture resembles breadcrumbs (or use your fingertips). Mix in the peanuts, then slowly add the water to form a dough.

3 Dust a work surface with a little flour and roll out the pastry to 2–3mm thick. Cut it into 4 circles large enough to line the base and sides of the cases and gently press the pastry into the prepared cases. Trim off any excess pastry with a knife, saving the scraps in case you need to fill any tears. Line with parchment paper, then fill with baking beans.

4 Preheat the air fryer to 160°C. Bake for 15 minutes, then remove from the air fryer and tip out the baking beans. Bake for a further 5–6 minutes until golden brown. Set aside to cool.

5 To make the filling, roughly chop the chocolate into small pieces and place in a bowl. Heat the cream until just boiling, then pour it over the chocolate. Cover the bowl with clingfilm or a plate and leave to stand for a few minutes. Mix using a wooden spoon until the chocolate has fully melted, then stir in the golden syrup. Pour the ganache into the tartlet cases and chill for 20–30 minutes until set.

6 Decorate with fresh berries or edible flowers and gold leaf just before serving, if liked.

TIP

You can bake the tartlet pastry cases up to 3 days ahead. Store well-wrapped in the fridge, or freeze the cases either raw or baked.

CHEAT'S DANISH PASTRIES – 3 WAYS

Short of time? Let's face it, who isn't?! You can make delicious Danish-style pastries in a flash by using ready-made all-butter puff pastry. I've given you three flavour options to choose from, so make one or all three if you're having a large gathering. Just don't tell anyone you cheated – they will never know!

**MAKES ABOUT
36 PASTRIES**
PREP: 60 MINUTES
BAKE: 20 MINUTES

Apricot custard Danish pastries

320g sheet of ready-rolled all-butter puff pastry

1 tbsp custard powder

1 tbsp caster sugar

200g milk

Flour, for dusting

1 medium egg, beaten

240g can apricot halves (6 halves are needed)

2 tsp granulated or caster sugar

3 tbsp apricot jam

Raisin swirls

320g sheet of ready-rolled all-butter puff pastry

1 tsp ground cinnamon

1 tsp ground ginger

50g caster sugar

100g soft butter

120g raisins

Flour, for dusting

1 medium egg, beaten

3 tsp apricot jam

For the apricot custard Danish pastries

1   Line baking trays or air fryer baskets with parchment paper, or use silicone liners.

2   Put the custard powder and sugar in a bowl. Add about 2 tablespoons of the milk and stir to form a paste. Heat the remaining milk until just boiling, then pour it over the paste. Mix with a whisk to eliminate any lumps. Return to the saucepan and heat over a medium heat, stirring continuously until thickened, then pour the custard back into the bowl, cover with clingfilm and leave to cool.

3   Unroll the pastry onto a lightly floured work surface. Cut it into six equal squares, then cut each square almost to the centre from each corner. Fold one point over to meet the centre and press with your finger. Miss the next corner, then pick up the following point and repeat, pressing into the centre to create a pinwheel/ Catherine wheel shape. Brush with egg wash.

4   Put 2 teaspoons of custard in the centre of each piece of pastry and nestle an apricot half on top. Sprinkle with sugar.

5   Preheat the air fryer to 160°C. Bake for 18–20 minutes, or until as golden as you like. Remove the parchment paper from underneath after about 12 minutes to allow the air to circulate and crisp up the bottoms.

6   Meanwhile, gently heat the jam with a little water to loosen. Glaze the pastries while still warm.

For the raisin swirls

1   Line baking trays or air fryer baskets with parchment paper, or use silicone liners.

2   In a bowl, beat the spices and sugar into the butter until soft and creamy. Mix in the raisins.

Pecan and maple twists

320g sheet of ready-rolled all-butter puff pastry

150g pecans

30g butter, melted

3 tbsp maple syrup, plus extra for glazing

Flour, for dusting

3 Unroll the pastry onto a lightly floured work surface. Spread the raisin mixture all over the pastry. Roll up into a sausage from one of the short sides. Chill for 30 minutes.

4 Slice into 12 equal discs. Flatten out each disc with the palm of your hand to a thickness of about 8mm (¼in) and place onto the prepared tray or basket. Brush with a little egg wash.

5 Preheat the air fryer to 160°C. Bake for 18–22 minutes, or until as golden as you like. Remove the parchment paper from underneath after about 12 minutes to allow the air to circulate and crisp up the bottoms.

6 Meanwhile, gently heat the jam with a little water to loosen. Glaze the pastries while still warm.

For the pecan and maple twists

1 Line baking trays or air fryer baskets with parchment paper, or use silicone liners.

2 Blitz the pecans to a fine crumb. In a bowl, mix the butter and maple syrup together, then tip in the nuts and stir to mix.

3 Unroll the pastry onto a lightly floured work surface. Cut the pastry in half lengthways to give you two equal rectangles. Brush each piece of pastry with egg wash. Spread the nut mixture over one piece and top with the second piece, egg wash face-down, to sandwich the filling. Chill for 30 minutes to firm up.

4 To make the twists, cut the stuffed pastry in half, then cut each half into eight thin strips to create 16 strips. Hold each strip at either end and twist in opposite directions to create a spiral, allowing the filling to show. Place onto the prepared tray or basket and brush over each twist with egg wash.

5 Preheat the air fryer to 160°C. Bake for 15–20 minutes, or until as golden as you like. Remove the parchment paper from underneath after about 12 minutes to allow the air to circulate and crisp up the bottoms. Brush with extra maple syrup while warm.

Adaptations

(DF) *Substitute the butter for vegan block butter or spread.*

(GF) *Switch the pastry for a gluten-free version.*

QUICK APPLE TART

Your friends will think you bought this tart from a posh French patisserie! It's just stunning with the glistening caramelised apple slices circled around the top and surrounded by crisp pastry. This works brilliantly in the air fryer, and is gorgeous served warm with ice cream or as it comes at room temperature.

SERVES 6–8
PREP: 15 MINUTES
BAKE: 20 MINUTES

320g ready-rolled puff pastry, preferably all-butter

60g butter

2–3 large eating apples (I used Cox's)

1 tsp vanilla extract or bean paste

1 tbsp caster sugar, plus a little extra for sprinkling

Juice of 1 lemon

2 rounded tbsp apricot jam

Vanilla ice cream or crème fraîche, to serve

1   Cut the pastry into a 25cm (10in) circle, or into whichever shape you like (see Tip). Place onto a sheet of parchment paper.

2   Slowly melt the butter in a saucepan. Meanwhile, core and thinly slice the apples. Toss the apple slices in the butter, adding the vanilla, sugar and lemon juice. Arrange the slices over the pastry, leaving a 2cm (¾in) clear border all round. Use your thumb and forefinger to crimp up the pastry edges to make a rim to stop the juices running off.

3   Preheat the air fryer to 190°C. Bake for 15–20 minutes until the apples are tender and the pastry crisp. Keep an eye on the apples – they should be a deep, dark golden colour at the edges. Remove the paper for the last 5 minutes once firmly set to allow the air to circulate underneath and crisp up the base.

4   Warm the jam and brush over the apples and pastry edge. Serve hot with vanilla ice cream or crème fraîche.

Adaptations

(DF) *Substitute the butter for vegan block butter or spread and use a dairy-free puff pastry.*

(GF) *Substitute the pastry for gluten-free puff pastry.*

TIP
This tart can be made into two smaller ones, if you have a two drawer style air fryer. Cut the pastry so that it fits inside your air fryer, leaving a 1cm (¾in) gap all around the tray so that the pastry doesn't go soggy. Halve the quantities above and follow the method above and bake for 15 minutes.

EASY STRAWBERRY TART

The mascarpone in this recipe gives these tartlets an almost strawberry tiramisu vibe. In Italian, tiramisu literally translates as a cheer-me-up, or pick-me-up, and these tarts won't let you down!

MAKES 1 LARGE TART

PREP: 30 MINUTES
CHILL: 30 MINUTES
BAKE: 21 MINUTES

For the pastry

180g plain flour, plus extra for dusting

90g unsalted butter, chilled and cubed, plus extra for greasing

¾ tsp sea salt

1 medium egg yolk

About 2 tbsp ice-cold water

For the filling

375g full-fat mascarpone cheese

225g double cream

3 tbsp icing sugar

2 tsp vanilla extract or bean paste

450g strawberries, hulled and sliced

2 heaped tbsp strawberry jam, sieved

A few mint leaves, thinly sliced

1 Lightly grease a 24cm (9in) tart tin.

2 Start by making the pastry. In a food processor blitz the flour, butter and salt together until the mixture resembles breadcrumbs. Add the egg yolk and a dash of ice-cold water – just enough for the mixture to form into clumps – do not over-process. If doing by hand, mix in the egg yolk and water using a cold knife. There's no need to rest the pastry.

3 Roll out the pastry to a 3–4mm (¼in) thickness, then line the prepared tin, gently pushing the pastry into the sides. Trim off the excess pastry. Keep the offcuts to patch up the potential odd tear or hole. Refrigerate for at least 30 minutes or freeze for 15 minutes. Prick the base with a fork and line the case with parchment paper and baking beans.

4 Preheat the air fryer to 160°C. Bake for 13–15 minutes, then remove the beans and bake for a further 5–6 minutes, or until as golden and crisp as you like. Place onto a wire rack to cool in the tin. Remove from the tin once cooled completely.

5 To make the filling, put the mascarpone, cream, icing sugar and vanilla in a bowl and whisk by hand until slightly thickened. Spoon the filling into the case and level the top. Arrange the strawberries in a decorative pile on top of the filling.

6 In a small saucepan, heat the jam with 2 teaspoons of water and gently bring to the boil. Leave to cool, then brush the glaze over the strawberry slices and sprinkle with the mint.

Adaptations

(GF) *Substitute the flour for a gluten-free blend, or use gluten-free pastry.*

Fast forward

Use shop-bought shortcrust pastry instead of making your own.

TIP
To get ahead, line
the case with pastry
up to 2 days in advance.
Wrap well and keep in the
fridge. Or freeze for up to a
month and blind bake from
frozen – they will need a
few more minutes in
the air fryer.

APRICOT TART

I think apricots are seriously underrated. They work well in this recipe, from underripe to slightly overripe, if you want to use fresh ones, so it's a good way of using up the apricots you bought with all good intentions of eating on their own as a healthy snack. I've used the canned kind for this tart; they are always perfectly ripe and bake really well.

MAKES 20CM (8IN) TART (SERVES 8–10)

PREP: 30 MINUTES
BAKE: 25 MINUTES

For the pastry

See recipe on p104

For the filling

60g unsalted butter, at room temperature, plus extra for greasing

50g golden caster sugar

½ tsp vanilla extract

1 medium egg

40g self-raising flour

30g ground almonds

¼ tsp baking powder

Pinch of sea salt

6 canned apricot halves or peach slices (or canned cherries are lovely too)

2 tbsp apricot jam, warmed

Icing sugar, for dusting

1 Lightly grease a 20cm (8in) round loose-bottom flan tin.

2 Prepare and bake the pastry as described on p104.

3 To make the filling, put the butter, sugar and vanilla in a bowl and whisk for 1–2 minutes using an electric hand mixer, or 3–5 minutes by hand until pale and fluffy. Beat in the egg, then stir through the flour, ground almonds, baking powder and salt.

4 Spoon the filling into the pastry case and spread over the base. Push in the apricot halves, flat-side down, to cover the whole surface.

5 Preheat the air fryer to 170°C. Bake for 20–25 minutes. Transfer to a wire rack to cool completely. Brush with the warmed apricot jam to glaze and dust with icing sugar.

Adaptations

(DF) *Substitute the butter for vegan block butter or spread.*

(GF) *Substitute the flour for a gluten-free blend, or use gluten-free pastry.*

Fast forward

Use shop-bought shortcrust pastry.

> **TIP**
> *You can make six tartlets instead of one large tart. The bake time for the tart and tartlets is about the same, but check on them a few minutes earlier just in case.*

CHERRY HAND PIES

These crispy cherry-filled pies are inspired by those McDonald's ones! They used to fry them years ago, when I was a teenager, and they were so good, but I believe they bake them now... or maybe they air fry them. Well, if they don't already, they should! Baking these in the air fryer is far healthier than deep frying them but doesn't scrimp on flavour. They are so quick to whip up you'll be enjoying them in no time! To make them a bit fancier for a pudding, serve them cut in half with a scoop of ice cream. I'm lovin' it!!!

MAKES 4 PIES

PREP: 10 MINUTES
BAKE: 25 MINUTES

320g sheet of ready-rolled puff pastry

Plain flour, for dusting

2 tbsp milk, for glazing

100g cherry pie filling

1 tbsp melted butter

2 tsp Demerara sugar

1   Line a baking tray with parchment paper, or use a silicone liner.

2   Unroll the pastry sheet onto a lightly floured work surface and cut into 4 equal rectangles. Brush the edges with milk.

3   Divide the cherry filling into 4 equal portions. Spoon along one long side of each rectangle, leaving a 1cm (½in) outer border clear along the filling side. Fold the bare bit of the pastry over the filling and use a fork to crimp the joined edges together.

4   Brush the tops with melted butter and sprinkle over the sugar. Make a small steam hole in the middle of the pies. Transfer to the prepared baking tray or basket.

5   Preheat the air fryer to 180°C. Bake for 15 minutes until golden and puffed up. Turn the pies over, brush the undersides with the rest of the butter and sprinkle with more sugar. Bake for a further 7–10 minutes until golden.

6   Transfer to a wire rack to cool for 10 minutes (the filling will be molten when it first comes out of the air fryer) and serve warm with a scoop of vanilla ice cream, or serve at room temperature. The pies will keep for 2 days in an airtight container.

CHOUX BUNS

These choux buns work best if your air fryer has a bake setting. Don't worry if it doesn't though; they'll still turn out fine, but may not be as uniform as air fryers can be a bit blowy, so they might be throwing some shapes in the baskets! I love choux pastry; it's so delicate and crisp, and not too sweet – a perfect vehicle for cream and seasonal fruit or chocolate. They are my sister's favourite too, served with lots of chocolate!

MAKES ABOUT 12 CHOUX BUNS
PREP: 30 MINUTES
BAKE: 25 MINUTES

For the choux pastry

40g whole milk

40g butter

10g caster sugar

Pinch of sea salt

80g strong while bread flour

110–115g beaten eggs (about 2 medium/large eggs)

For the Chantilly cream filling

150g double cream

10g icing or caster sugar

½ tsp vanilla extract or bean paste

For the chocolate topping

100g melted dark or milk chocolate, for dipping

Gold leaf, if you're feeling fancy

1   Line a baking tray or air fryer baskets with parchment paper, or use a silicone liner.

2   Start by making the choux pastry. In a saucepan, bring the milk, butter, sugar, salt and 40g of water to the boil. Add the flour all in one go and beat well with a wooden spoon. Cook out for 1–2 minutes.

3   Place the mixture in a bowl or electric stand mixer and leave to cool for 5 minutes. Beat in the eggs a little at a time until combined and the mixture is of a good dropping consistency but still holds its shape. It shouldn't be too runny, so don't add all the eggs at once. Transfer to a piping bag fitted with a 1cm round nozzle and leave to rest for 5–10 minutes. Pipe walnut-sized balls onto the prepared tray or directly into the prepared baskets, leaving enough space in between as they will double in size. Pat down any peaks with a damp finger.

4   Preheat the air fryer to 180°C. Bake for about 20 minutes until deep golden brown and completely crisp. Pierce the top and bottom of each choux bun with a cocktail stick or the tip of a sharp knife. Turn them over to release the steam and return to the air fryer for a further 2 minutes to crisp off the bottoms. Transfer to a wire rack to cool completely.

5   To make the Chantilly cream filling, put all ingredients in a bowl and whisk to soft peaks. Cut the choux buns in half, fill the bottom half with cream, dip the top half in the melted chocolate and place onto the filling. Decorate with gold leaf if desired.

JAM TARTS

A simple, trusty recipe that goes back generations – just ask the Queen of Hearts! These little jam tarts are a bit like cookie cups, as the pastry is sweet and biscuit-like. I love these filled with strawberry or raspberry jam, but the choice is yours.

MAKES ABOUT 16 TARTS

PREP: 30 MINUTES
CHILL: 1 HOUR
BAKE: 17 MINUTES

175g plain flour, plus extra for dusting

75g icing sugar

½ tsp sea salt

115g unsalted butter, chilled and cut into cubes, plus extra for greasing

2 medium egg yolks, chilled

A dash of ice-cold water, only if needed (I used 15g; depending on the size of the yolks, you might not need it)

About 150g of your favourite jam

1 Grease as many 7cm (3in) round, 2cm (¾in) deep tartlet moulds as you have (you'll have to do this in batches), or if you have a larger oven style air fryer use a jam tart tin.

2 Put the flour, icing sugar and salt in a food processor and pulse a few times to mix. Add the butter and blitz until the mixture resembles breadcrumbs.

3 Add the egg yolks and blitz again. If the dough doesn't come together, add a few drops of ice-cold water until it just starts to come together, but don't overmix. Once a dough begins to form, tip it out and bring it together into a ball with your hands. Flatten out to a disc and wrap in clingfilm. Chill for about 30 minutes.

4 Lightly flour a work surface, then roll out the dough (I used guide sticks), dusting the top of the dough too. Then roll out even thinner until you have a sheet of pastry about 3mm thick.

5 Use a round cutter to cut out circles large enough to line the base and sides of your moulds. Press the circles in gently. Reroll the scraps to make more tartlets. Prick the bases with a fork. Chill for a further 30 minutes or freeze for 10–15 minutes before baking.

6 Preheat the air fryer 160°C. Line the pastry cases with parchment paper and fill with baking beans. Bake for 10 minutes, then remove the beans and paper and bake for a further 4 minutes. Spoon in the jam and bake for a further 3 minutes.

7 Leave to cool completely before serving.

MUM'S QUICHE

This is a classic quiche recipe and a family favourite. Mum used to make a few flavours – roasted onions, mushrooms, asparagus, and the classic bacon and cheese. My sister and I always had plenty of clonks (her word for slices!) when we were little, with bacon and cheese, but I'm veggie now, so for this version I use my favourite veggie bacon. When my mum used to bake these she'd make a few and freeze them, and any excess pastry she'd give to me and my sister to make little biscuits with. We loved making them and eating them warm from the oven.

MAKES 20CM (8IN) QUICHE OR 6 TARTLETS
PREP: 30 MINUTES
CHILL: 30 MINUTES
BAKE: 1 HOUR

For the pastry (for either size)

180g plain flour, plus extra for dusting

90g unsalted butter, chilled and cubed, plus extra for greasing

¾ tsp sea salt

1 medium egg, plus 1 yolk

About 2 tbsp ice-cold water

For the filling (if making a large quiche)

225g double cream

3 medium eggs

120g strong Cheddar, grated

75g veggie bacon (or regular), chopped, fried and drained

1 tbsp chopped chives (optional)

Freshly ground black pepper

1   Lightly grease a 20cm (8in) round fluted tin, or six 10cm (4in) tartlet cases.

2   Start by making the pastry. In a food processor, blend the flour, butter and salt together until the mixture resembles breadcrumbs. Add the egg and yolk and a dash of ice-cold water – just enough for the mixture to form into clumps – do not over-process. If doing by hand, rub the flour and butter with your fingertips and mix in the egg yolk and water with a cold knife.

3   Roll out the pastry immediately to 3–4mm thick and line the tin or cases, pushing the pastry into the fluted edge. Trim off the excess pastry, keeping the scraps in case of the odd tear or hole you may need to patch up, then refrigerate for at least 30 minutes before baking. Prick the base(s), then line them with parchment paper and baking beans.

4   Preheat the air fryer to 160°C. Bake for 15–20 minutes until the case(s) begin to colour and dry out. The tartlets will take slightly less time to bake – just keep your eye on them as they may need a couple of minutes less.

5   Remove the beans and bake for a further 10 minutes for the large case, and 5–6 minutes for the small cases, or until as golden and crisp as you like.

6   To make the filling, beat the cream and eggs together with plenty of black pepper. Scatter the base(s) with half the cheese, then sprinkle over the cooked bacon. Pour over the remaining cream and egg mixture and top with the remaining cheese. Sprinkle with chives, if using.

recipe continued overleaf . . .

For the filling (if making 6 tartlets)

150g double cream

2 medium eggs

Freshly ground black pepper

120g strong Cheddar, grated

75g veggie bacon (or regular), chopped, fried and drained

1 tbsp chopped chives (optional)

7 Bake the large quiche for 25–30 minutes and the tartlets for 10–12 minutes until risen, puffy and deeply golden brown. Allow to cool for 10–15 minutes before serving, or allow to cool completely and serve cold or at room temperature.

Adaptations

(GF) *Substitute the flour for a gluten-free blend, or use gluten-free pastry.*

Fast forward

Use shop-bought shortcrust pastry instead of making your own.

TIPS

• *If you want to get ahead, you can line the cases with pastry up to 2 days in advance. Just wrap them in clingfilm and keep them in the fridge. You can also freeze them for up to a month and blind bake from frozen, but they will need a few more minutes in the air fryer.*

• *If you want to keep the pastry extra crisp once baked and before filling, brush the case(s) with beaten egg and return to the air fryer for a further minute.*

LEEK, CHEESE AND POTATO PIE

This is a delicious slab pie made with ready-rolled puff pastry. It's a fun pie to make and no dish is needed – simply load up the pastry and bake directly on a baking sheet. The filling is encased in pastry, so there's plenty of crunch. Serve with greens or a side salad. If you have a smaller air fryer, quarter the pastry to make two smaller pies.

SERVES 2–3

PREP: 30 MINUTES
CHILL: 30 MINUTES
BAKE: 30 MINUTES

1½ tbsp olive oil

2 leeks, thinly sliced (yielding about 200g)

½ tsp sea salt, plus extra to taste

1 garlic clove, finely chopped or crushed

2 tsp fennel seeds

A few sprigs of thyme

180g boiled/precooked potatoes, sliced

1 medium egg

100g strong Cheddar, crumbled (or any hard cheese)

1 tbsp Dijon mustard

375g sheet of ready-rolled puff pastry

1 egg, beaten, to glaze

Freshly ground black pepper

1 Line a baking sheet or air fryer basket with parchment paper, or use a silicone liner.

2 Heat the oil in a large frying pan over a low–medium heat. Fry the leeks with the salt for 10–15 minutes, stirring regularly, until very soft and lightly browning. Add the garlic and fennel seeds and cook for a further minute, then stir in the thyme. Remove from the heat.

3 Transfer to a large bowl. Add the potatoes, egg, cheese and mustard. Season with salt and plenty of black pepper, mixing well to combine, then chill while you prepare the pastry.

4 Unroll the sheet of pastry, and cut it in two, making one half 2.5cm (1in) wider than the other.

5 Place the filling in the centre of the smaller rectangle of pastry, pressing down to neaten with clean fingers, and leaving a 3cm (1in) border all round. Brush the with egg wash, then top with the larger piece of pastry. Press gently over the filling to encase and press the edges with a fork dipped in flour to seal. Brush all over with more egg wash and chill for 30 minutes (or you can do this the day before).

6 Preheat the air fryer to 180°C. Place a sheet of foil underneath the baskets or vented trays in case of any leakage. Bake for 25–30 minutes until crisp and golden. Cool slightly and serve with salad or greens.

Adaptation

GF *Use a gluten-free pastry.*

Fast forward

Use tinned potatoes and slice them up.

VEGETABLE ROSE TARTS

By rolling up thinly sliced and precooked vegetables, the flowery effect of these mini tartlets is second to none! You need a bit of patience, but the final result is well worth it. Encased in a light and buttery Parmesan pastry, these mini tartlets are absolutely spot on for a light lunch served with a salad, or for entertaining friends and family at gatherings.

MAKES 12 TARTS
PREP: 45 MINUTES
CHILL: 30 MINUTES
BAKE: 27 MINUTES

For the pastry

250g plain flour, plus extra for dusting

125g butter, chilled and cubed, plus extra for greasing

30g Parmesan, grated

1 egg yolk

Freshly ground black pepper

For the filling

200g baby carrots (I used mixed colours)

200g baby courgettes

75g sundried tomatoes, chopped

125g mascarpone cheese

1 medium egg

75g green pesto

25g Cheddar, grated

25g Parmesan, grated

Sea salt and freshly ground black pepper

1   Grease two six-hole cupcake tins, or use individual silicone moulds.

2   Start by making the pastry. Blitz the flour and butter in a food processor until the mixture resembles breadcrumbs. Add the Parmesan, egg yolk and a generous grind of pepper. Blitz briefly, adding a little cold water, until a dough forms. Tip out onto a lightly floured work surface and roll out to a large, thin sheet about 4mm (¼in) thick. Using a cutter, cut out circles large enough to line the base and sides of the cupcake holes. Gently press in and neaten, then refrigerate for at least 30 minutes.

3   Cut squares of parchment paper and scrunch them up slightly. Nestle inside each pastry case and fill with baking beans. Preheat the air fryer 170°C. Bake for 10 minutes, then remove the paper and baking beans and bake for a further 5 minutes.

4   Meanwhile, make the filling. Thinly slice the carrots and courgettes lengthways to make strips. I use a mandoline to do this, but you can use a vegetable peeler, too. Put them in a bowl, season to taste, cover with water and microwave for a few minutes until soft and bendable, or boil in a saucepan for about 2 minutes. Refresh in cold water, drain, then dry on paper towels.

5   Combine the remaining filling ingredients in a large bowl until creamy, then spoon 1 tablespoon into each pastry case. Roll up a couple of the sliced vegetables to form a spiral for the centre of each tart. Continue wrapping vegetable slices to form a rose effect, overlapping them towards the edge of each tart case.

6   Preheat the air fryer to 160°C. Bake for 10–12 minutes until the filling has set and the veggies are browning. Leave to cool for 5 minutes before serving, or serve at room temperature.

7   These will keep for 3 days in the fridge. They can be gently reheated in the air fryer on 140°C for about 10 minutes.

Adaptation

(GF) *Substitute the flour for a gluten-free blend.*

TOMATO GALETTE

This is a delicious easy tart, gorgeous served warm or at room temperature with a salad. If you have a large oven-style air fryer you can make one large galette, but if you have a smaller single-basket air fryer, you can halve the quantities and make one smaller free-form tartlet to fit your basket or tray.

MAKES 1 LARGE GALETTE OR 2 SMALLER ONES (SERVES 6–8)

PREP: 1 HOUR 20 MINUTES

BAKE: 50 MINUTES

150g tomatoes of your choice

1 tsp sea salt, plus extra to taste

75g strong Cheddar, grated

1 tbsp chopped oregano or thyme, or a mix

1 egg, beaten, to glaze

Freshly ground black pepper, to taste

For the pastry

180g wholemeal spelt flour (or plain flour), plus extra for dusting

100g unsalted butter, chilled and diced

1 tsp sea salt

1 medium egg, beaten

1 Slice the tomatoes to 5mm (¼in) thick. Put them in a colander set over a large bowl and sprinkle over the salt. Set aside for 1 hour to draw out the juices.

2 If you have an oven-style air fryer, line a baking sheet with parchment paper. If using the basket kind, cut two pieces of parchment paper to fit the baskets, with an overhang of 5cm (2in) to help lift the galettes (or use silicone liners).

3 To make the pastry, tip the flour, butter and salt into a food processor and blitz to fine breadcrumbs. Add the egg and pulse to a soft dough – if the dough seems dry, add ½ teaspoon of cold water at a time until it comes together.

4 Knead the pastry briefly, pat into a round, and roll it out on a lightly floured work surface. Before the pastry is fully rolled out, transfer it to the prepared baking sheet and continue rolling out to a rectangle approximately 28x24cm. If making two smaller galettes, make the bases slightly smaller than the basket and liner so the steam can escape. This will prevent soggy bottoms.

5 Add half the cheese, arrange the tomatoes in an even layer, then sprinkle with thyme and the remaining cheese, leaving a border of about 5cm (2in) around the edge. Season with salt and pepper.

6 Brush the pastry border with egg wash, then fold the border up so it slightly overlaps the filling. Brush with more egg wash.

7 Preheat the air fryer to 160°C. Bake for 45–50 minutes for the large galette, 30–35 minutes for the smaller ones. The pastry should be golden and crisp, the tomatoes soft and browning. Remove the parchment paper and allow the base to crisp up for the last 5–10 minutes. Leave to stand for 5–10 minutes.

8 Serve warm, garnished with fresh herbs, with a side salad.

Adaptation

GF *Switch the pastry for a gluten-free version.*

TIP
You can use any seasonal fillings you like! For instance, switch the tomatoes for fried sliced onions and mushrooms, and use your favourite cheese.

ROASTED TOMATO AND MOZZARELLA PUFF PASTRY TART

This is a wonderful tart to make in the summer when there's an abundance of all sorts of heritage tomatoes. I love the Isle of Wight ones. The lush sweetness of roasted tomatoes and the creamy mozzarella are a match made in heaven, married with buttery and crisp puff pastry. This open tart is perfect as a starter or main course, eaten at room temperature al fresco with a side salad.

SERVES 4–6

PREP: 15 MINUTES
BAKE: 37 MINUTES

250g ripe tomatoes, halved or quartered

Olive oil

375g sheet of ready-rolled puff pastry

2 tbsp green pesto

150g mozzarella, sliced and torn into rough pieces

1 egg, beaten, to glaze

Handful of fresh basil leaves

Sea salt flakes and freshly ground black pepper

TIP
You can make two smaller tarts by cutting the pasty in half and splitting the ingredients equally between the two. Bake for 15–18 minutes.

1   Preheat the air fryer to 200°C.

2   Put the tomatoes in the air fryer basket or tray, drizzle with a little oil and season with salt and black pepper. Cook for 10–15 minutes, mixing halfway through, until softened and beginning to caramelise. Set aside.

3   Unroll the pastry onto a flat baking sheet and use a sharp knife to very lightly score around the edge of the pastry, leaving a 2cm (¾in) border all round. Prick the pastry all over the inside of the marked edge with a fork. Spread over the pesto, then arrange the mozzarella and tomatoes over the top. Season and drizzle with a little oil. Brush the border with egg wash.

4   Preheat the air fryer to 180°C. Bake for 18–22 minutes until the pastry is crisp and risen, the tomatoes are soft and the mozzarella is golden. Scatter over the basil leaves. Serve warm or at room temperature with a green salad.

Adaptations

Ⓖ *Substitute the pastry for a gluten-free version.*

Ⓟ *Use vegan puff pastry, pesto and cheese, and glaze with plant milk instead of egg.*

TAPENADE PALMIERS

Also known as palm leaves, elephant or pig's ears or butterflies. Call them what you will but these palmiers make me think of Princess Leia! I love the salty tapenade in this savoury version of a French favourite. The cheese is optional, but I have cheese with just about everything, so I'm keeping it in! This recipe makes double the quantity of tapenade you need for the palmiers, so you can have the rest in sandwiches or for dipping. It will keep in the fridge for a week, or it can be frozen too.

MAKES 18–20 PALMIERS

PREP: 10 MINUTES
CHILL: 30 MINUTES
BAKE: 18 MINUTES

Flour, for dusting

375g sheet of ready-rolled puff pastry

40g strong hard cheese, such as Parmesan or pecorino, grated

For the tapenade

175g black pitted olives

40g capers

1 garlic clove, crushed

2 tsp chopped thyme

2 tsp chopped flat-leaf parsley

Juice of ½ lemon

75g extra virgin olive oil

1 Line a baking tray with parchment paper, or use a silicone liner.

2 Put all the tapenade ingredients, except the oil, into a food processor or blender. Blitz until chunky, then add the oil and blitz to a paste, leaving some bits as you don't want a completely smooth texture.

3 Unroll the pastry sheet onto a floured work surface. Spread half the tapenade over the pastry using a spoon or cranked palette knife, then sprinkle over the cheese. Roll the pastry sheet up from both short sides into the centre, to make two rolls that join in the middle.

4 Wrap in clingfilm and chill for about 30 minutes to firm up, or make the day before if you're getting ahead for entertaining. Cut the pastry into 1cm (½in) thick slices and pop on the prepared tray or basket, leaving space between each as they will expand and puff up.

5 Preheat the air fryer to 180°C. Bake for 16–18 minutes until deep golden and puffy. Turn over to cook the underside if needed for the last couple of minutes.

Adaptation

(GF) *Substitute the pastry for a gluten-free version.*

Fast forward

Swap the tapenade for shop-bought tapenade, or green or red pesto.

SAUSAGE ROLLS

Who doesn't love a sausage roll? No party is complete without them... and they make a great quick lunch or dinner served with baked beans! These sausage rolls are super-easy to make in the air fryer. You can use regular sausage meat or any veggie sausages. Adding the onion and fresh herbs packs even more flavour into these tasty, flaky favourites. They are seriously addictive!

MAKES 9 SMALL SAUSAGE ROLLS
PREP: 20 MINUTES
CHILL: 20 MINUTES
BAKE: 25 MINUTES

---

2 tsp vegetable oil

1 small (about 75g chopped weight) white onion, finely chopped

1 garlic clove, crushed

50g panko or dried white breadcrumbs

2 tsp chopped thyme

2 tsp chopped sage

2 tsp tomato purée

½ tsp sea salt

½ tsp white pepper

300g sausage meat (regular or veggie)

375g sheet of ready-rolled puff pastry

Flour, for dusting

1 egg, beaten (or plant milk), to glaze

1 Line a baking tray with parchment paper, or use a silicone liner.

2 Heat the oil in a frying pan and gently soften the onion on a low–medium heat for 8–10 minutes until translucent. Add the garlic and cook for a few more minutes. Set aside to cool.

3 Put the breadcrumbs, herbs, tomato purée and seasoning into a large bowl. Stir in the cooked onion and garlic, then add the sausage meat (remove the meat or veggie filling from their casings) and use your hands to mix everything together.

4 Unroll the pastry onto a lightly floured work surface. With the pastry landscape, not portrait, cut across to make three pieces approx. 12x8cm (5x3in).

5 Divide the sausage meat into 3 equal portions. Shape it along one long edge of each rectangle. Brush the empty strip next to the filling with egg wash or milk. Fold the pastry over the filling to cover, then seal together with a fork dipped in flour. Slightly flatten the rolls, then refrigerate for 20 minutes to firm up.

6 When ready to bake, cut each length into 3 equal pieces, so that you have 9 sausage rolls. You can freeze some at this point. Brush with egg wash or plant milk and pop on the prepared tray or in the basket, leaving a bit of space between each.

7 Preheat the air fryer to 160°C. Bake for 20–25 mins until the pastry is deep golden and crisp, and the filling is cooked through. Serve warm, at room temperature or cold.

8 The sausage rolls will keep for up to 3 days in the fridge.

Adaptations

(PB) *Substitute the pastry for a vegan version and use vegan sausages and dairy-free plant-based milk.*

SPINACH AND FETA SWIRLS

These swirls were made for air fryers! They bake perfectly, and are so crisp and buttery. My top tip is to bake them in small individual round dishes or moulds so that they don't unravel, or spear through them with a skewer to hold them in place if baking on a tray. They make a magnificent buffet centrepiece, a real feast for the eyes!

MAKES 4 SWIRLS
PREP: 25 MINUTES
BAKE: 30 MINUTES

350g baby spinach, washed

1 tbsp olive oil

1 large onion, finely chopped

200g feta cheese, crumbled

50g Cheddar, grated

½ tsp dried oregano

Grating of nutmeg

4 sheets of shop-bought filo pastry

50g salted butter, melted

Freshly ground black pepper, to taste

1 Heat a large non-stick pan over a medium heat. Tip in the spinach and cook, stirring, until wilted (you don't need any oil or water as it will steam in its own moisture). Leave to cool a little, then tip into a clean tea towel and squeeze out as much water as possible. Chop and transfer to a bowl.

2 Heat the oil in a non-stick frying pan. Fry the onion for about 10 minutes until softened. Tip into the bowl with the spinach, then stir in both cheeses using a fork until fully combined. Add the oregano and nutmeg, taste for seasoning and add a grinding of black pepper, if liked.

3 Lay a sheet of filo on a work surface. Brush with a little melted butter, then spoon about 4 tablespoons of the filling in a line along the longest edge of the pastry. Roll loosely into a sausage (don't roll it too tight as this might cause the pastry to split), then coil the pastry up and skewer it to keep the coil in place if baking individual swirls on a tray (or contain each swirl into a 10–12cm (4–5in) round dish. Repeat with the remaining filo sheets and filling. If your air fryer allows, nestle all four swirls into a tray that fits the swirls and your air fryer. Brush each swirl with a little melted butter.

4 Preheat the air fryer to 180°C. Bake for 25–30 minutes until crisp and as deep golden as you like. Serve warm or at room temperature.

TIP
If you have a large oven-style air fryer you can double the quantities for a large swirl pie in a 22cm (9in) round dish. You'll need 7 filo sheets, with the filling divided equally still. Place your first roll in the centre, then place the rest around it to fit snugly in the tin for a large swirl. Bake for 30 minutes.

BROCCOLI CHEESE PUFFS

These puffs are super-quick and easy to make and are ideal as a filling snack, or serve them for lunch or dinner with your favourite sides (I like mine with baked beans). I also love to make these with asparagus when it's in season, but sprouting broccoli is fab and available all year round, so give both versions a go.

MAKES 6 PUFFS
PREP: 15 MINUTES
BAKE: 18 MINUTES

200g Tenderstem broccoli

2 tsp olive oil

375g sheet of ready-rolled puff pastry or all-butter puff pastry

1 medium egg, beaten

240g Swiss cheese or 12 ready-cut slices (Emmenthal or Leerdammer style)

2 tsp clear honey

Chilli flakes, for sprinkling

Sea salt and freshly ground black pepper, to taste

1 Line a baking sheet with parchment paper if using an oven-style air fryer. If using an air fryer with drawers, the puffs will go directly on the trays.

2 Blanch the broccoli for 2 minutes, then refresh in cold water. Toss in the oil to coat, and season with salt and pepper.

3 Cut the pastry into six 12x8cm (5x3in) rectangles and brush with egg wash. Place one slice of cheese diagonally on top of each pastry rectangle. Top with broccoli, then another slice of cheese. Take opposite corners of the pastry and bring them to the centre to join to make a parcel, with either end open. Seal the corners at the centre, pressing gently, and brush with egg wash. Place the puffs on the prepared baking sheet or trays.

4 Preheat the air fryer to 160°C. Bake for 10–12 minutes, then remove the paper so that the air can circulate and crisp up the base.

5 Drizzle a little honey over the puffs, sprinkle with chilli flakes and return to the air fryer for a further 4–5 minutes until puffed up and turning golden brown. Flip the puffs over to cook the bottoms for an extra minute, if needed. Serve immediately.

PUDDINGS & DESSERTS

MINI COOKIES 'N' CREAM CHEESECAKES

I love baked cheesecakes – the texture, the creaminess and the fact they aren't too sweet make them a delicious bake. These adorable little desserts are ideal sweet treats for parties or afternoon tea. The contrast with the dark biscuit base and cookies studding through the white filling is gorgeous. They keep for up to 5 days, so they are ideal to get ahead and bake for gatherings or dessert. Have all ingredients at room temperature before baking.

MAKES 8 MINI CHEESECAKES

PREP: 20 MINUTES

CHILL: 4 HOURS

BAKE: 20 MINUTES

35g butter, melted

130g Oreo cookies, blitzed or bashed to fine crumbs, plus extra 50g, chopped

180g full-fat cream cheese

80g white caster sugar

1 tsp vanilla extract or bean paste

2 medium eggs

75g soured cream

Pinch of sea salt

Mini Oreo cookies, for the topping

Vanilla ice cream, to serve

1   Line a muffin tin with paper cases, or use individual silicone moulds.

2   In a bowl, mix the melted butter into the crumbled cookies and divide equally between the 8 muffin cases. Use the bottom of a glass or similar to flatten the base.

3   Beat the cream cheese with an electric mixer for about 2 minutes. Gradually add the sugar and beat until combined, then add the vanilla. Add the eggs one at a time, beating well after each addition, and scrape down the side of the bowl as needed. Beat in the soured cream and salt and fold through the chopped cookies. Divide the batter equally between the muffin cases, filling each almost to the top.

4   Preheat the air fryer to 135°C. Bake, rotating halfway through, for 16–20 minutes until just set.

5   Leave to cool in the tin, then refrigerate for at least 4 hours or overnight. Place a mini Oreo cookie (or a broken full-size one) on top of each cheesecake. Serve as they come or with vanilla ice cream. They will keep in the fridge for up to 5 days.

NEW YORK BAKED CHEESECAKE

This is my husband's favourite cake, and it's probably my second favourite (after Christmas cake!). We always go to Eileen's Cheesecakes in New York when we visit, and we have the gorgeous mini cheesecakes from there and eat them in the park across the block. I love this cake because it's not too sweet and the air fryer bakes it really well.

MAKES 20CM (8IN) ROUND CAKE (SERVES 10–12)

PREP: 15 MINUTES

CHILL: 30 MINUTES

BAKE: ABOUT 1 HOUR

For the base

200g digestive biscuits

85g butter, melted and cooled

2 tsp caster sugar

For the topping

130g caster sugar

1½ tsp cornflour

¼ tsp sea salt

540g full-fat cream cheese, at room temperature

1½ tsp vanilla bean paste

3 medium eggs

95g soured cream, at room temperature

1 Line a 20cm (8in) springform tin with parchment paper.

2 Start by making the base. Blitz the biscuits in a food processor, then add the melted butter and sugar and pulse a few times to mix. Alternatively, put the biscuits in a plastic food bag and bash with a rolling pin as finely as you can and transfer to a bowl before adding the butter and sugar.

3 Tip into the prepared tin and press down over the base with your fingers or the bottom of a glass, until the base is compact and flat, but taking care not to knock the paper about on the side. Refrigerate while you make the topping.

4 To make the topping, mix the sugar, cornflour and salt together in a large bowl. In a separate bowl or using a stand mixer, beat the cream cheese and vanilla until smooth, soft and creamy, or cream by hand with a wooden spoon. Then gradually beat in the sugar mixture, a tablespoon at a time until incorporated.

5 Add the eggs one at a time, beating on a slow–medium speed for about 20 seconds until incorporated. Add the soured cream and beat again. Remove the cake tin from the fridge and pour the topping into the tin.

6 Preheat the air fryer to 135°C. Put a sheet of foil under the tin in case some of the butter leaks out while baking. Bake for about 50 minutes, checking every so often. If browning too quickly, reduce the temperature to 130°C. Take care pulling the basket in and out as the topping is delicate and may crack.

7 Cook for a further 10 minutes if needed – the top and edges should be turning golden brown. Don't overbake the cheesecake. The topping should still have a little wobble as it will set as it cools.

8 Once baked, turn off the air fryer and allow to cool completely in the air fryer (this prevents the cheesecake from cracking). Refrigerate overnight. Carefully remove the cheesecake from the tin. It is best eaten the day after baking and will keep in the fridge for up to 5 days.

PEACH AND RASPBERRY COBBLER

This comforting pudding is perfect served with lashings of custard for those cold, wintry evenings or just as good served with ice cream in the summer. Have it on Christmas Day for all I care – Santa certainly won't stop you! The topping is dead easy to make, so it's great for a last-minute dessert. Peaches and raspberries make a perfect pairing, but you can swap these fruits to your liking. The cobbler topping works so well on top of any cooked fruits, so swap for what's in season or in your cupboard.

SERVES 4

PREP: 10 MINUTES

BAKE: 35 MINUTES

410g can peaches, drained and sliced

Couple of handfuls of fresh or frozen raspberries

120g golden caster sugar, plus extra for sprinkling

175g self-raising flour

Pinch of sea salt

150g butter, chilled and cubed, plus extra for greasing

1 medium egg

1 tsp vanilla extract or bean paste

Custard or vanilla ice cream, to serve

1   Grease a 20x15cm (8x6in) baking dish. Arrange the peach slices on the base and scatter over the raspberries. Sprinkle over 2 tablespoons of the sugar and set aside.

2   Tip the flour, remaining sugar and salt into a food processor. Whizz to combine, then add the butter, pulsing until the mixture resembles breadcrumbs (or rub with your fingertips). Add the egg and vanilla and blitz to a thick dough, or mix by hand with a butterknife and bring together in a thick, sticky dough.

3   Spoon the dough in dollops on top of the fruit, leaving small gaps for the dough to spread into. Sprinkle with a little more sugar.

4   Preheat the air fryer to 170°C. Bake for 30–35 minutes until deep golden. Serve with custard or scoops of vanilla ice cream.

TIP
Swap the peaches for other canned fruits, if liked. Apricots, pears and plums work well, and use blackberries in place of raspberries.

SYRUP SPONGE PUDDINGS

These individual syrup sponge puddings are such a comforting treat, and they are special because you get one all to yourself. I always used to steam mine, but these bake so well in the air fryer. You can use traditional mini aluminium pudding basins, if so grease well, but silicone moulds, which are perfect for air fryers, work best. Don't fill them more than three-quarters full as they really rise when they bake and you don't want them to spill over. They will sink back as they cool.

MAKES 4–6 PUDDINGS

PREP: 15 MINUTES
BAKE: 22 MINUTES

150g self-raising flour

½ tsp baking powder

¼ tsp sea salt

200g golden syrup

Juice and finely grated zest of 1 lemon

140g unsalted butter, softened, plus extra for greasing

140g golden caster sugar

1 tsp vanilla extract or bean paste

2 medium eggs

75g milk

Ice cream or custard, to serve

1 Grease four or six pudding basins depending on the size (I used 175ml capacity ones) or use silicone moulds. Smaller/larger moulds will make two more/two fewer puddings.

2 Put the flour, baking powder and salt in a bowl and dry mix to combine.

3 In a separate bowl, mix the golden syrup with the lemon juice, zest and 1 tablespoon of water.

4 Using a stand mixer or electric hand mixer, cream the butter, sugar and vanilla until pale and fluffy, or cream by hand with a wooden spoon. Add the eggs one at a time, beating well after each addition. Add the dry ingredients in two batches, mixing between each addition until just combined. Add the milk and give a final light mix (be careful not to overmix as the sponge will become tough).

5 Divide the syrup mixture equally between the basins or moulds. Carefully dollop the batter over the syrup base. Start by going around the outside edge and work inwards to trap the syrup underneath. Alternatively, load the batter into a piping bag and pipe around the edge above the syrup, winding inwards and filling to about three-quarters full. Smooth over with the back of a spoon. Chill and bake the next day, or bake straight away.

6 Preheat the air fryer to 160°C. Bake for 20–22 minutes until golden brown, well risen and cooked through. The sponge will rise slightly over the top but will shrink down after baking.

7 Leave in the basins for 5–10 minutes to settle and firm up a little, then carefully invert and release onto a plate or bowl to reveal the tender, glistening, wobbly sponge. Serve with ice cream or custard, or both!

8 Any leftovers can be kept in the fridge for a few days and reheated, or frozen too.

JAM SPONGE PUDDING

School wouldn't have been the same without a sponge pudding swimming in custard! I almost feel that they don't taste the same unless served on a white, plastic food tray. Like fish and chips in newspaper!

SERVES 4
PREP: 15 MINUTES
BAKE: 50 MINUTES

200g jam (I love raspberry or strawberry jam)

100g very soft butter, plus extra for greasing

90g golden caster sugar

100g self-raising flour

½ tsp baking powder

2 medium eggs

1–2 tbsp milk

1 tsp vanilla extract or bean paste

Ice cream or custard, to serve

1 Generously grease a 20x15cm (8x6in) baking dish.

2 Stir the jam until smooth, then spoon it into the baking dish, smooth the surface to form an even layer.

3 Beat the remaining ingredients together until smooth, then carefully pour over the jam, completely covering it to create ` an even layer.

4 Preheat the air fryer to 150°C. Bake for 45–50 minutes until the sponge is light, golden and risen, and a skewer inserted into the centre comes out clean. Serve with ice cream or custard. Any leftovers can be kept in the fridge for a few days and reheated.

Adaptations

(DF) *Substitute the butter for vegan block butter or spread and use a dairy-free plant-based milk.*

(GF) *Substitute the flour for a gluten-free blend.*

TIP
Using the same quantities, you can make four individual puddings, if you prefer. Use four 10cm (4in) ramekins and bake for 30–35 minutes.

SELF-SAUCING STICKY TOFFEE PUDDING

I was lucky enough to go to the world-famous Pudding Club in the Cotswolds for my TV show, Beautiful Baking, for an evening of pure indulgence, where they parade eight puddings and you can try them all! They did a wicked sticky toffee one, and this is my homage to the Pudding Club as it's my favourite (and my kids' favourite, too!) This is just what you want for after Sunday lunch; it's the ultimate comfort food.

SERVES 3–4
PREP: 15 MINUTES
BAKE: 30 MINUTES

For the sponge

75g dried pitted dates, roughly chopped

½ tsp bicarbonate of soda

100g boiling water

50g butter, melted, plus extra to grease

75g dark muscovado sugar

2 medium eggs

50g whole milk

125g self-raising flour

Pinch of sea salt

For the sauce

125g dark muscovado sugar

125g double cream

1   Grease a 19x15cm (7.5 x6in) baking dish with butter.

2   Start by making the sponge. Put the dates in a small heatproof bowl. Sprinkle with the bicarbonate of soda and pour over the boiling water. Allow to soften for 10 minutes.

3   Meanwhile, in a small saucepan over a low heat, mix the sauce ingredients together with 60g of water until the sugar dissolves, then remove from the heat and set side.

4   Tip the dates into a food processor or blender and blitz a couple of times, then add the remaining sponge ingredients. Whiz to a thick batter, scraping down the sides so everything is fully incorporated. There should still be some flecks of date in the batter. Tip into the prepared baking dish, then slowly pour the sauce over the top – it is easier to pour the sauce into the corners of the dish.

5   Preheat the air fryer to 150°C. Bake for 25–30 minutes. Check with a skewer, being careful not to poke all the way through to the sauce (the sauce sinks under the sponge). The sponge should be risen and firm, and the sauce bubbling underneath. Allow to cool for 5 minutes and serve with cream or ice cream.

PAVLOVA

Yes, unbelievably you can bake pavlova in the air fryer! This recipe is made using the Swiss meringue method: it's worth heating the egg whites and sugar to create a perfect crisp shell and soft mallow centre. This recipe makes a large pavlova, but if you have a smaller air fryer you can pipe individual mini ones, or make meringue kisses! You can bake the shell up to 5 days in advance – just keep it sealed in a large food bag so it's completely airtight. All it then takes is 5 minutes to whip up some cream and prep the topping and you have an impressive pudding, so it's a great one to make ahead if you're entertaining.

SERVES 6–8
PREP: 20 MINUTES
BAKE: 1½ HOURS

For the meringue

3 egg whites, at room temperature

150g white caster sugar

¾ tsp white vinegar

50g white chocolate

For the topping

100g double cream

2 tsp icing sugar (optional)

1 tsp vanilla extract

About 150g mixed fruits or berries of your choice

1   Start by making the meringue. Put the egg whites into a heatproof bowl. Add the sugar and vinegar and set the bowl over a saucepan of simmering water. Make sure the base of the bowl doesn't touch the water.

2   Use a balloon whisk and beat the egg whites and sugar to encourage the sugar to dissolve. This will take a few minutes – use your fingertips to check the consistency. If the mixture feels gritty, then continue to cook and whisk over the pan. When ready, the mixture should feel warm and slippery/silky smooth between your fingertips.

3   Remove the bowl from the heat and use an electric hand mixer to whisk on high speed until the meringue holds firm peaks – this can take 10 minutes or more. The meringue should be stiff and glossy.

4   If you want to be super neat, draw a 20cm (8in) circle on a piece of parchment paper (subject to the size of your air fryer) and place the paper in the air fryer basket. Fit a piping bag with a 1cm star tip (Wilton 1m) and fill the bag with the meringue. Hold the piping bag over the paper at a 45-degree angle and pipe a ring of meringue around the outer pencil line, using a spiral motion to create a rope effect, then fill in towards the centre. Then go back around the outer edge in a swirly style to create the height (alternatively, you can spoon the meringue into the lined basket in one mound, then spread it out and create a well in the centre, lifting the spoon on and off the top of the meringue ring to create little peaks). If you have an oven-style air fryer, do this on a baking sheet and slide it in.

recipe continued overleaf . . .

5   Preheat the air fryer to 120°C. Bake for 30 minutes, then reduce the temperature to 100°C and bake for a further 50 minutes–1 hour. Turn off the heat and leave in the air fryer to cool completely. If making ahead, melt the chocolate and paint the inside of the cooled pavlova and allow to set, then store until needed.

6   When ready to fill, put the cream, icing sugar, if using, and vanilla in a bowl and whisk until the cream holds soft peaks. Fill the meringue with the cream, top with the fruit and serve immediately.

Adaptations

(DF) *Substitute the double cream for whippable dairy-free plant-based cream and use dairy-free chocolate.*

TIP
Line the cooked pavlova with 50g melted white chocolate (or your preferred chocolate) if you want it to stay crisper for longer. This will stop the cream dissolving the meringue. It's best to leave filling the meringue with cream and fruit until just before serving.

BLACKBERRY CRUMBLES

A hug in a ramekin and a real winter warmer. I can envisage myself sitting in a high-backed Chesterfield chair by an open stone fireplace while tucking into one of these made with blackberries I've picked from my garden. Bliss! I live in London though, so for now I'll have to make do with blackberries from the local supermarket. But we do have a very nice log burner at home. Now where's my tartan blanket?

MAKES 4–6 CRUMBLES

PREP: 15 MINUTES
BAKE: 20 MINUTES

For the filling

650g blackberries

2 tbsp cornflour

125g golden
caster sugar

Juice of 1 lemon

For the crumble

80g porridge oats

45g tahini (well stirred)

170g self-raising flour

125g butter, chilled, cut
into small cubes, plus
extra for greasing

110g Demerara sugar

½ tsp sea salt

1   Grease 4–6 ramekins.

2   Start by making the filling. Put the blackberries, cornflour, sugar and lemon juice in a bowl and mix with a spoon, then set aside for the fruit to release its juices.

3   To make the crumble, put the oats in a bowl and stir in the tahini with a spoon to evenly coat. Set aside.

4   In a separate bowl, rub the flour and butter together, or blitz in a food processor, then stir in the sugar, oat mixture and salt until you get a coarse, lumpy crumble. Divide the berries between the prepared dishes and level off. Top with the crumble and completely cover the fruit.

5   Preheat the air fryer to 180°C. Bake for 18–20 minutes until deep golden brown. Leave to cool slightly, then serve warm with ice cream.

GIANT COOKIE PIE

This giant cookie pie is my air fryer version of those huge warm skillet cookies. They are delicious, with a chewy gooey cookie dough centre but sweet and crisp on the outside. These are perfect for a gathering or party, sliced warm with some ice cream. You can even turn these into a birthday cookie by adding a message onto the top, which makes a fun alternative to a cake!

SERVES 4

PREP: 15 MINUTES
BAKE: 22 MINUTES

125g unsalted butter, softened, plus extra for greasing

150g soft light brown sugar

50g caster sugar

2 tsp vanilla extract

1 medium egg

250g self-raising flour

25g cornflour

½ tsp sea salt

150g chopped chocolate or chips (I love half white and half milk, but use whatever you like)

TIP

If you want to make a smaller 15cm (6in) cookie, halve the quantities. Use a 15cm (6in) round tin and bake for 15–17 minutes.

1 Grease and line a 20cm (8in) round tin, or use a silicone mould.

2 Using a stand mixer or electric hand mixer, cream the butter, both sugars and vanilla until pale and fluffy, or cream by hand with a wooden spoon. Mix in the egg.

3 In a separate bowl, combine the flour, cornflour and salt. Mix into the wet mixture. Add the chocolate chips and mix thoroughly. Flatten the dough into a circle about 20cm (8in) in diameter directly into the prepared tin, flattening with a damp palm or rubber spatula to level and neaten.

4 Preheat the air fryer to 160°C. Bake for 20–22 minutes until cooked through and turning golden and crisp on the edges but still squidgy inside. Leave to cool in the tin for about 5 minutes, then carefully turn out.

5 Slice and serve warm with cream or ice cream. If making ahead, you can pop the slices in the microwave for 10–15 seconds to gently warm up (or wrap in foil and reheat in the air fryer on 100°C for a couple of minutes).

Adaptations

(DF) *Substitute the butter for vegan block butter or spread. Also, substitute the chocolate for a dairy-free version.*

(GF) *Substitute the flour for a gluten-free blend.*

CROISSANT BREAD AND BUTTER PUDDING

This recipe is another flexible friend. Simply use any leftover croissants, whatever the flavour, then put your own spin on it! I love a chocolate and hazelnut combo. Or just add Nutella. Or how about using almond croissants and adding cherry jam? Peanut butter, Biscoff spread, lemon curd and raspberries – anything goes with this recipe!

SERVES 4–6
PREP: 15 MINUTES
SOAKING: 30 MINUTES
BAKE: 22 MINUTES

3 medium eggs

1 tsp vanilla bean paste

40g caster sugar

200g milk

275g double cream

4–5 leftover croissants

50g butter, plus extra for greasing

100g hazelnut creme spread

200g milk chocolate chips

Demerara sugar, for sprinkling

Ice cream or custard, to serve

1 Grease a 20x15cm (8x6in) baking dish.

2 In a large bowl, whisk the eggs, vanilla and sugar together. Stir in the milk and cream.

3 Slice the croissants in half lengthways, butter the cut sides, then spread with hazelnut creme. Add a layer of croissants to the dish, pour over half the liquid and scatter with half the chocolate chips. Add another layer of croissants, crusty sides uppermost, and pour over the remaining liquid and chocolate. Leave to soak for about 30 minutes.

4 Preheat the air fryer to 160°C. Sprinkle with a little Demerara sugar and bake for 18–22 minutes, or until deep golden.

5 Serve warm, with ice cream or custard.

TIP
If you'd rather make individual puddings, grease four to six 8–10cm (3–4in) ramekins or moulds. Bake for 18-22 minutes.

CHOCOLATE FONDANTS

These gooey chocolatey desserts are notoriously difficult to get right. Timing is key, but with the simplicity of an air fryer, fear no longer! These little beauties will come out perfect every time – spongy on the outside, slightly biscuity on top, and smooth and silky on the inside. This is a knockout pud to serve after dinner to impress your friends. You can get ahead with these and make them the day before, leave in the fridge or even freeze them, and bake from chilled or frozen.

MAKES 4 FONDANTS

PREP: 20 MINUTES
CHILL: 1 HOUR
BAKE: 9 MINUTES

20g butter, melted, for greasing

7g cocoa powder, plus extra for dusting

100g dark chocolate, roughly chopped

100g butter

75g golden caster sugar

2 medium eggs

½ tsp vanilla extract

75g plain flour, sifted

Vanilla ice cream, clotted cream, whipped cream, mascarpone or crème fraîche, to serve

1   Generously brush four 7.5cm (3in) pudding moulds with the melted butter, then refrigerate for 15 minutes to set the butter. Or use silicone moulds.

2   Brush the moulds with more butter, then dust with the cocoa powder, rolling and tipping the moulds to completely coat the base and sides. Shake off any excess cocoa powder into a bowl. Refrigerate the moulds again while you make the batter.

3   Put the chocolate and butter in the microwave and heat in 30-second bursts, stirring in between until smooth and glossy, or melt in a bain-marie. Set aside.

4   Beat the sugar and the eggs for about 5 minutes with an electric whisk until tripled in volume, very pale and fluffy and the whisk leaves trails over the surface. Whisk in the vanilla. Gently fold through the melted chocolate and butter, then fold through the sifted flour and leftover cocoa powder, taking care not to knock the air out of the mixture.

5   Divide the mixture equally between the moulds and leave to set in the fridge for at least 1 hour. Alternatively, you could make them the day before, or freeze them for up to a month.

6   Preheat the air fryer to 170°C. If you have an oven-style air fryer, place a baking tray in the air fryer; otherwise lower them directly into the baskets. Carefully place the moulds onto the hot baking tray or baskets and bake for 9 minutes from chilled (or 12–14 minutes from frozen), or until the mixture slightly shrinks away from the edges of the moulds and the tops are crusting over. Remove from the air fryer and leave to stand for 1 minute, then run a knife around the top edges to loosen and invert onto serving plates.

7   Serve with vanilla ice cream, clotted cream, whipped cream, mascarpone or crème fraîche.

BREAD & DOUGH

GARLIC AND HERB CHEESY BABKA BREAD

All the twirls and swirls in this bread are packed with juicy, savoury magnificence. A kaleidoscope of flavour. It's the perfect tear-and-share garlic bread for a gathering. Just don't stare at it for too long.

MAKES 1 BABKA, OR TWO SMALLER ONES

PREP: 25 MINUTES
BAKE: 40 MINUTES

For the dough

150g whole milk

325g white bread flour, plus extra for dusting

2 tsp caster sugar

1½ tsp sea salt

7g sachet fast-action dried yeast

1 medium egg

80g unsalted butter, very soft, plus extra for greasing

For the filling

100g salted butter, softened

4–5 garlic cloves, crushed

1 tbsp olive oil

Handful each of flat-leaf parsley and basil, finely chopped

125g block of mozzarella, grated

25g Parmesan, finely grated

Freshly ground black pepper

For dusting

Polenta or semolina, to dust the tin

1 Grease a 20cm (8in) round tin with butter and dust with polenta or semolina, or use a silicone mould.

2 Start by making the dough. Heat the milk in a small saucepan over a low heat until warm but not hot.

3 Put the flour, sugar and salt in a large bowl, or the bowl of a stand mixer, and mix through. Add the yeast and mix again. Add the warm milk, egg and butter and bring together with a spatula or your hand in a claw until you get a very sticky, shaggy dough.

4 Knead the dough for about 8 minutes in a stand mixer or 10–12 minutes by hand until completely smooth and pliable. If kneading by hand, you might find it easier to mix and knead the dough in the bowl. Scrape the dough into a large oiled bowl, cover with a clean tea towel and leave to rise for about 1½–2 hours, or until doubled in size. After this time, refrigerate the dough for 30 minutes to make it easier to roll out and fill.

5 To make the filling, mix together the butter, garlic, oil, herbs and a good grinding of black pepper.

6 Remove the dough from the fridge. Roll it out on a lightly floured work surface to a 40x30cm (16x12in) rectangle. Spread the flavoured butter evenly over the dough using a spatula or palette knife, then sprinkle over the mozzarella and Parmesan.

7 With the longest side closest to you, roll the dough up into a tight, long sausage. Transfer to a board, seam-side down, and cut in half lengthways so you have two long pieces. With both lengths of dough parallel to one another, cross them over each other in a plaited style. Carefully coil up into a spiral and lift into the prepared tin. Cover with a tea towel to prove for 1 hour.

8 Preheat the air fryer to 160°C. Bake for 35–40 minutes, or until deep golden. If needed, turn over for the last 5 minutes to make sure the bottom is cooked, then flip back over and bake for a further minute. Cool in the tin for 10 minutes, then flip out onto a wire rack and cool until just warm and ready for slicing.

FLUFFY DINNER ROLLS

I'm so lucky that in my lifetime we've had many American adventures, including living out there for a period. They often serve soups and salad with fluffy 'dinner rolls' that are so soft and squishy and pretty addictive. I set about making my own version, and in recent years have started using the tangzhong method for some of my breads, and I fully recommend doing this even though it might sound strange if you've not heard of it before. It's a bit scientific, but put simply, what you do is cook a bit of flour with water or milk until it becomes a thick paste, which is then added to the rest of the ingredients to make the dough. It makes the bread softer, helps it stay moist and last longer.

MAKES 9 ROLLS

PREP: 25 MINUTES
BAKE: 30 MINUTES

For the tangzhong

25g strong white bread flour

135g whole milk

For the dough

150g cold milk

20g caster or granulated sugar

40g butter, softened

1½ tsp sea salt

300g strong white bread flour

7g sachet fast-action dried yeast

Oil, for greasing

1 medium egg, beaten, to glaze

Sea salt flakes

1   If you have an oven-style air fryer, line a 23cm (8in) square tin with parchment paper. Otherwise, line the air fryer baskets with parchment paper or use individual silicone moulds to make single rolls.

2   Start by making the tangzhong. Put the flour in a small saucepan and gradually whisk in the milk on a low–medium heat. Whisk constantly for 3–4 minutes to avoid getting any lumps, until the mixture has thickened to a paste or pudding-like consistency. Remove from the heat.

3   To make the dough, gradually add the cold milk into the tangzhong, whisking so no lumps form, and transfer to the bowl of a stand mixer fitted with a dough hook or into a large bowl. Make sure the mixture isn't too hot; it should be just warm, so as not to kill the yeast.

4   Add the sugar, butter, salt, flour and yeast. Stir to form a rough dough, then set the stand mixer on medium speed and mix for about 10 minutes until the dough is smooth and bouncy (up to 15 minutes if kneading by hand).

5   Put the dough in a lightly oiled bowl, cover with a tea towel and refrigerate to rise overnight, or leave in a warm place for 1–2 hours until doubled in size. When the dough has proved, knock it back and give it a brief 30-second knead to knock out the air.

6   Divide the dough into 9 equal pieces and shape into balls. You can either arrange them in the tin as balls and let them rise like this, or if you want a swirly style, roll each ball out into a long oval, then fold one-third over the middle along the length, then

recipe continued overleaf . . .

the other third over the top to form a long, narrow packet. Then roll up from one end into a little roll and place seam-side down and spaced out in rows in the tin as they will almost double in size when they rise and bake.

7   Loosely cover with a tea towel and leave to rise for 45 minutes–1 hour until puffy. If you gently press the dough with your finger it should spring back slowly, and maybe leave a slight indentation. If it springs back quickly, then it needs a little longer. Keep an eye on the rolls as the rise will depend on the yeast and the room temperature. Brush the rolls with egg wash and sprinkle with sea salt flakes.

8   Preheat the air fryer to 160°C. Bake for 15–20 minutes. Remove the rolls from the paper after this time and cook for a further 5–10 minutes so the bases crisp up. Allow to cool in the tin or baskets for 5 minutes, then carefully transfer to a wire rack and leave to cool for about 20 minutes before serving warm. To reheat, return to the air fryer on 120°C for about 3 minutes.

9   The rolls can be frozen for up to a month, but are best eaten freshly baked.

Adaptations

(DF) *Substitute the butter for vegan block butter or spread. Also, substitute the milk for unsweetened plant milk (soy is best).*

TIP
You can put the rolls in the fridge to slow prove for a few hours if you want to get ahead and just bake them later when dinner is served. They will keep for 3–4 hours in the fridge.

BREAKFAST BAPS

My husband loves my baps for breakfast. These should really be called All-day baps.
Make them in batches to freeze and just reheat them in the air fryer when needed.
My kids often have these with vegan burgers or vegan bacon and ketchup after a
night out. The smell wafting up the stairs at 1am makes my mouth water!

MAKES 8 BAPS

PREP: 25 MINUTES
BAKE: 15 MINUTES

375g strong white
bread flour, plus
extra for dusting

1½ tsp sea salt

10g caster sugar

7g sachet fast-
action dried yeast

30g butter, softened

300g tepid water

Oil, for oiling

1   Line a baking tray with parchment paper, or use a silicone liner.

2   Put the flour in a large bowl with the salt and sugar. Dry mix then
    add the yeast and mix again.

3   Add the butter and most of the water (you may not need all
    the water), and drag through the mixture with your fingertips,
    gradually incorporating the flour until you have a soft, but not
    soggy dough. You can do this in a stand mixer fitted with a
    dough hook, if you have one.

4   Tip the dough out onto a lightly floured work surface and knead
    it for 8–10 minutes until silky and smooth, or knead in the stand
    mixer for 5–6 minutes.

5   Put the dough in an oiled bowl, cover with clingfilm and leave to
    rise in a warm place or proving drawer for about 1 hour, or until
    doubled in size.

6   Once risen, divide the dough into 8 equal pieces and shape into
    loose balls by rolling the dough with your hands. Set aside on a
    floured work surface, cover with a clean tea towel and leave to
    rest for 15 minutes.

7   Using a rolling pin, gently flatten each ball and place onto the
    prepared trays or into the baskets. Leave enough space between
    each roll as they will puff up. Loosely cover the trays or baskets
    with oiled clingfilm or a tea towel and leave to prove in a warm
    place for 45 minutes until risen and almost doubled in size.

8   Preheat the air fryer to 180°C. Dust the surface of the rolls with
    extra flour, then bake for about 15 minutes until risen and golden
    brown. Leave to cool on the trays or in the baskets for 5 minutes,
    then transfer to a wire rack to cool completely.

9   The baps are best eaten fresh on the day, or can be stored in
    a food bag and refreshed in the air fryer on 140°C for a few
    minutes. They can be frozen for up to a month.

EASY 50/50 LOAF

If you have a large oven-style air fryer that can accommodate a 900g (2lb) loaf tin, including the rise, you can make a large loaf. The bread will rise up very tall so do make sure you have the oven shelf low. Otherwise, cut the dough in half and make two 450g (1lb) loaves, or use 15cm (6in) round silicone moulds to create two round loaves. You can make rolls with the dough if you prefer.

MAKES 900G (1LB) LOAF

PREP: 20 MINUTES
BAKE: 40 MINUTES

250g strong wholemeal bread flour

250g strong white bread flour

10g sea salt

7g sachet fast-action dried yeast

325–350g tepid water

50g butter, melted

Oil, for greasing

Polenta or semolina, for dusting (optional)

TIP
Rub a little oil onto your hands before shaping the dough to avoid sticking.

1   Oil a 900g (1lb) loaf tin then dust it with polenta or semolina, if using (this is optional, but gives the base of the loaf a lovely crunch and prevents sticking).

2   Put both flours in a large bowl or stand mixer bowl and mix in the salt. Add the yeast and mix again. Bring together with the tepid water and melted butter until the mixture resembles a shaggy, slightly sticky porridge.

3   Knead in the stand mixer fitted with a dough hook for 8–10 minutes or by hand for about 15 minutes until you get a springy, bouncy, elastic dough. Put the dough in an oiled bowl and leave to rise until doubled in size. Knock back the dough and tip it onto a work surface.

4   Lay the dough so that it's portrait rather than landscape and then in the top third, then fold the bottom third to cover the two folded pieces, then roll this up lengthways in a tight spiral, fold the ends under the dough to neaten, lift up and place into the tin so it's all neatly tucked in, with the smooth part of the dough uppermost and the joins inside the tin.

5   If making two smaller loaves, split the dough in half and shape each half as described above, then pop into the tins. Cover with oiled clingfilm or a clean tea towel and allow to rise again until puffed up and sitting proud of the tin.

6   Preheat the air fryer to 180°C. Bake the large loaf for 35–40 minutes. The smaller loaves will need 30 minutes. If you want a little more colour, increase the temperature to 190–200°C for the last 5 minutes. Bake until the base sounds hollow when tapped. Resist slicing if you can for at least 30 minutes!

Adaptation

DF *Substitute the butter for vegan block butter, spread or olive oil.*

SODA BREAD

I love soda bread. My mother-in-law got me into it 25 years ago. We used to buy it from a lovely health-food shop called Greens in Leigh-on-Sea. It's still there today, owned by Richard Green and his family. It's so quick and easy to make, and making it in the air fryer speeds up the baking time even more. You can have a tasty crusty loaf or rolls in no time.

**MAKES 1
LARGE LOAF**

PREP: 10 MINUTES

BAKE: 35 MINUTES

375g strong wholemeal and mixed grains bread flour (I used Cotswold Crunch, but regular wholemeal is good, too), plus extra for dusting

1½ tsp sea salt

¾ tsp bicarbonate of soda

300g buttermilk

A little milk, if needed

Oats, for topping (optional)

1 Lightly flour a baking sheet, or use a silicone liner.

2 Tip the flour, salt and bicarbonate of soda into a large bowl and stir. Make a well in the centre and pour in the buttermilk, mixing quickly using a large fork to form a soft dough. Depending on the absorbency of the flour, you may need to add a little milk if the dough seems too stiff, however, it should not be too wet or sticky.

3 Turn the dough out onto a lightly floured work surface and knead briefly until it feels smooth and pliable. Form into a round loaf and flatten the dough slightly before placing it on the prepared baking sheet. Sprinkle the top with oats, if using, and cut a cross in the loaf.

4 Preheat the air fryer to 180°C. Bake for 30–35 minutes, or until the loaf sounds hollow when tapped on the underside. Transfer onto a wire rack to cool.

TIPS

• *You can make a smaller loaf by halving the ingredients. Bake for 20–25 minutes. Alternatively, you can make 8 bread rolls. Just divide the dough into 8 equal pieces, roll into balls and bake for 10–12 minutes.*

• *If you can't get hold of buttermilk you can easily make your own. Sour 300g of whole milk by adding 3 teaspoons of apple cider vinegar or lemon juice to it. It's that simple! Alternatively, use half natural yoghurt and half milk – stir together and leave to sour.*

OLIVE AND TOMATO BREADSTICKS

Who wants plain old breadsticks when you can flavour them with olives and tomato? They can be cut to any size – the more random and rustic the better – and served in glasses or jugs. They look like they are from a posh deli or straight out of Ottolenghi's window. A huge favourite with my grown-up kids, too, as we're always hosting gatherings with drinks and you need something to soak it all up!

MAKES ABOUT 30–40 BREADSTICKS

PREP: 20 MINUTES

BAKE: 10 MINUTES

250g strong white bread flour, plus extra for dusting

50g fine sea salt

½ 7g sachet fast-action dried yeast

2 tbsp chopped thyme

175–200g warm water

1 tbsp olive oil, plus extra for oiling

75g black and/or green olives, finely chopped

50g sundried or sun-blushed tomatoes, finely chopped

TIP

These are lovely served alongside some olive oil or dips, or the tapenade on p119.

1 Line a baking tray or air fryer baskets with parchment paper, or use a silicone liner.

2 Put the flour in the bowl of a stand mixer fitted with a dough hook attachment (or do by hand in a large bowl, but this will take more kneading time). Add the salt to one side of the bowl and the yeast to the other. Sprinkle over the thyme.

3 Add half the warm water and the olive oil and mix on a slow speed. As the dough starts to come together, gradually add the rest of the water (you may not need it all). Knead for 6–7 minutes on a medium–high speed. Once the dough is springy, tip it out onto a lightly floured work surface and stretch it out. Fold half the olives and half the tomatoes into the dough. Stretch out the dough again and press in the remaining olives and tomatoes, folding the dough over until well distributed.

4 Put the dough in an oiled bowl, cover with a clean tea towel and set aside for about 45 minutes, until doubled in size. The timing will depend on the yeast and the room temperature.

5 Tip the dough out onto a generously floured work surface and divide it into three pieces to make it easier to handle. If you've got a small air fryer, wrap two pieces in clingfilm and refrigerate while you roll out and bake the other piece. You'll need to bake the breadsticks in batches, but they don't take long.

6 Stretch out the dough and roll it into a large piece about 5–6mm thick. Dust the top with flour. Cut into thin random strips of different lengths that will fit in your air fryer – a pizza wheel is ideal for this. Place the lengths onto the prepared tray or baskets, leaving a little space between.

7 Preheat the air fryer to 200°C. Bake for 8–10 minutes until cooked through and golden. Turn over if needed to make sure both sides are cooked. Cool for as long as you can resist!

TIP
You can make two smaller loaves, if you prefer. Just divide the dough into 2 equal pieces, shape as for the large loaf and bake in air fryer baskets lined with parchment paper for 23–30 minutes. You can also make rolls. These will take 15–20 minutes to bake.

OVERNIGHT NO-KNEAD FRIDGE BREAD

No-knead bread is a fantastic option for those that want to enjoy homemade bread without the hassle of kneading. Quite often, people are put off making bread if they don't have a stand mixer as kneading by hand does take time and effort, so this is great to give a go if you have no special equipment. This recipe requires minimal time and effort. Shop-bought bread has so many unnecessary additives to help preserve it for weeks, whereas this bread has a handful of ingredients – no nasties in here!

MAKES 1 LARGE LOAF

PREP: 10 MINUTES
CHILL: OVERNIGHT
BAKE: 40 MINUTES

500g very strong white bread flour, plus extra for dusting

10g sea salt

7g sachet fast-action dried yeast

350–375g water

Olive oil, for oiling

A little melted butter

1 The evening before, put the flour in a bowl. Add the salt to one side of the bowl and the yeast to the other to avoid killing the yeast. Add the water and mix together with a spoon until you have a shaggy, porridge-like dough. It shouldn't be really wet, but it shouldn't be dry either. As it proves overnight, the dough will become bubbly and wetter. Cover the bowl with oiled clingfilm or a clean damp tea towel and refrigerate overnight.

2 When ready to bake, line a baking tray with parchment paper. Alternatively, you can place the loaf in a 20cm (8in) round silicone mould.

3 Flour a work surface and plop the bubbly dough onto it. You want to avoid playing about with it too much, or adding too much flour, so it's a good idea to oil your hands before handling the dough. Bring the dough together by lifting the outer edges into the centre to form a ball (use a dough scraper if you have one). Shape the dough into a tight ball, with the join facing down, flouring your hands if you need to, then place onto the prepared tray and leave to rest and rise for about 45 minutes, loosely covered with oiled clingfilm or a clean tea towel.

4 Preheat the air fryer to 200°C. Brush the dough with melted butter and slash the tops with a bread lame, knife or snip with scissors. Bake for 35–40 minutes.

5 Turn the bread over to brown and crisp the bottom for the last few minutes of the bake, if needed. Remove from the air fryer and place on a wire rack to cool, resisting slicing for at least 20 minutes, otherwise the dough will be too squidgy and tear.

6 The bread will keep for up to 5 days or can be sliced and frozen, ready for toasting.

FOCACCIA

This is the perfect recipe for baking directly in an air fryer basket. The focaccia should stretch out to a 22–25cm (9–10in) square. If you have a larger oven-style air fryer and a big crowd to feed like I do, you can double the quantities and bake in a 25x35cm (10x14in) baking or roasting tray.

MAKES 1 MEDIUM FOCACCIA

PREP: 15 MINUTES
BAKE: 25 MINUTES

250g very strong white bread flour, plus extra for dusting

7g sachet fast-action dried yeast

5g fine sea salt

About 200g lukewarm water

3–4 tbsp olive oil, plus extra for greasing and soaking once baked

Polenta or semolina (optional)

1–2 tsp sea salt flakes

Rosemary sprigs, whole garlic cloves or olives (optional)

1 Grease a 22cm or 25cm (9 or 10in) square tin with oil, or line the air fryer basket with parchment paper. Scatter with polenta or semolina (this is optional, but gives the base of the focaccia a lovely crunch and prevents sticking).

2 Tip the flour into a large mixing bowl or stand mixer fitted with a dough hook. Add the yeast to one side of the bowl and the salt to the other to avoid killing the yeast, then gently mix to combine.

3 Make a well in the centre of the flour. Mix 1 tablespoon of the oil into the warm water, then add it gradually to the flour until you have a wet and sticky dough (you may not need all the water, or perhaps you may need a little extra, as the absorbency of flours varies).

4 Knead on slow until the dough comes together, then increase the speed to medium–high for about 5 minutes until the dough is really springy and bouncy. If doing by hand, tip the dough onto a work surface and knead for 5–10 minutes until soft and less sticky. Avoid using flour when kneading so that the dough doesn't dry out. It should be a very hydrated dough.

5 Transfer the dough to a clean, lightly oiled bowl. Cover with a tea towel and leave to prove for about 1 hour, or until doubled in size. The timing will depend on the yeast and the room temperature.

6 Tip the dough out and stretch it out to the approximate size of your tin or air fryer basket, then lift it in. It will puff up and expand, so don't be too fussy about getting it completely stretched out. Brush or rub over a little more oil, then loosely cover with a tea towel or oiled clingfilm and leave to prove for a further 45 minutes–1 hour until really puffy and risen. The dough should be jelly-like and wobbly.

recipe continued overleaf . . .

7   Mix 2 tablespoons of the oil with 1 tablespoon of water and brush over the dough. Using your fingers, push into the dough until you can feel the bottom of the tin or basket to give that dimpled focaccia look. Sprinkle over the sea salt flakes and poke in extras like rosemary sprigs, garlic cloves or olives, if you like.

8   Preheat the air fryer to 180°C. Bake for about 20–25 minutes until golden. If you're able to, lift out the focaccia and turn it 180 degrees if you find your air fryer cooks a little more fiercely on one side. It should be crispy on the top and bottom. If it seems a bit wet and doughy, gently flip it over and bake for a further 3–4 minutes. Then turn it back over and bake for a further 1–2 minutes. The focaccia should be bubbly, deep golden brown and completely cooked through.

9   As soon as the focaccia comes out, drench it with more oil and water emulsion (2 tablespoons of oil mixed with 1 tablespoon of water) while still hot. Leave in the tin for 5 minutes.

10 Remove the focaccia from the tin and cut it into squares, or just tear it. We fight over it at our house – it's seriously addictive! It's delicious served warm, or you can have it cold with extra olive oil and balsamic vinegar, or use it when making toasted sandwiches. It will keep for about 3 days if well wrapped.

EASY FLATBREADS

These simple flatbreads are always a winning accompaniment for a curry or mezze. They're as good as if they'd just come out of a tandoor. They can be used as pizza bases, too, or as hot or cold wraps with your favourite fillings. This recipe is a twist on traditional bread-making with no need for yeast, combining a handful of simple ingredients.

MAKES 6 FLATBREADS

PREP: 5 MINUTES

BAKE: 8 MINUTES

250g self-raising flour, plus extra for dusting

½ tsp baking powder

250g natural yoghurt

2 tsp olive oil, or any oil

½ tsp sea salt

Melted butter or oil, for brushing

TIP

Lightly oil your hands before handling the dough to help prevent sticking.

1 Put all the ingredients, except the melted butter, in a bowl and bring together with a spoon or spatula, then use your hands to knead the mixture in the bowl until it comes together into a shaggy dough.

2 Tip out onto a lightly floured work surface and knead for 1–2 minutes until the dough feels smooth, pliable and lump free. Divide into 6 equal pieces, then roll into balls.

3 Dust the work surface again and roll the balls out into flatbreads; they should be 10–12cm (4–5in) in diameter. Leave on the surface to rest for a few minutes while you heat up the air fryer.

4 Preheat the air fryer to 200°C. Brush each flatbread with a little melted butter or oil on both sides and place onto the rack or basket. Bake for 7–8 minutes, flipping halfway through until turning golden and spotted and puffing up.

5 Serve warm to accompany a curry or salad, or with dips. If using as pizza bases, air fry them for 2 minutes on each side, then add your toppings of choice and bake for a further 3–5 minutes.

CHEESE-STUFFED GARLIC DOUGH BALLS

If you love stringy pizza-style cheese, this one is for you. This recipe makes one large sharing bread to fit in a 22cm (9in) tin or directly on an oven-style air fryer basket. For smaller machines, separate the balls into baskets and bake in batches of six. You can halve the quantities and keep the packet of yeast in the fridge once opened, sealed with a bag clip or in a food bag, for up to a month.

**MAKES 1 LARGE
SHARING
BREAD OR 11–12
DOUGH BALLS**
PREP: 30 MINUTES
BAKE: 30 MINUTES

50g polenta or semolina

11–12 mozzarella pearls
or chunks of mozzarella

For the dough

350g strong white
bread flour

1½ tsp sea salt

7g sachet fast-
action dried yeast

About 250g
warm water

For the garlic butter

100g butter

3–4 garlic cloves,
crushed

Handful of
chopped basil

Sea salt and freshly
ground black pepper

1   Start by making the dough. Put the flour and salt into a large bowl or stand mixer bowl and mix to combine, then add the yeast and start incorporating the warm water. Mix in the bowl with a bread scraper or using an oiled hand until the dough starts coming together, then tip the dough out onto a work surface and knead for about 15 minutes until the dough forms a smooth and springy ball. Alternatively, knead in the stand mixer for 5–6 minutes.

2   Transfer the dough to an oiled bowl, cover with a damp tea towel or oiled clingfilm, and leave in a warm place for 45 minutes–1 hour, or until doubled in size. The timing will depend on the yeast and the room temperature.

3   To make the garlic butter, melt the butter in a microwave-safe bowl or a saucepan, then stir in the garlic. Season with salt and black pepper, then stir in the basil. Set aside.

4   Generously brush a 23cm (9in) round tin with some garlic butter and scatter over the polenta or semolina (or line the air fryer baskets with parchment paper). If making two half batches place directly into a rectangular drawer or tin that fits your air fryer.

5   Once the dough has proved, knock it back, tip it onto the work surface and give it a little knead. Cut into 11–12 pieces weighing 45–50g. Roll each piece into a ball.

6   Flatten each ball slightly, press a mozzarella pearl in the centre, then bring the dough around to seal in the cheese and shape into a ball again. Place into the prepared tin or baskets, join-side down, leaving a little space between each as they will puff up and join up as they bake. Leave to prove again for 30–40 minutes.

recipe continued overleaf . . .

7   Preheat the air fryer to 160°C. Brush the dough balls with more garlic butter and bake for 18–20 minutes. After this time, remove them from the air fryer and brush with more garlic butter. Bake for a further 5–10 minutes until golden brown. If the balls need more colour, increase the heat to 180°C for the last 5 minutes. Make sure the dough balls are cooked on the underside; if they are a little doughy, carefully turn them over and bake for a further few minutes to crisp off the bottoms. Smaller batches will take less time.

8   Leave to cool for 5–10 minutes before serving with extra garlic butter or oil and sea salt flakes for dipping.

TIP
Leftover dough balls can be wrapped in foil and reheated in the air fryer at 140°C for a few minutes.

PIZZA PINWHEELS

Jazz up your margarita pizza slices and serve them as classy pinwheels instead. Triangles are so last year, darling!

MAKES 9–10 PINWHEELS

PREP: 20 MINUTES

BAKE: 25 MINUTES

450g strong white bread flour, plus extra for dusting

10g sea salt

7g sachet fast-action dried yeast

300g tepid water

1 tbsp olive oil, plus extra for oiling

1 tbsp fine polenta or semolina, plus extra for dusting

175g pizza sauce

100g mozzarella, grated

25g Parmesan, grated

2 tbsp of chopped basil (optional)

½ tsp pizza herbs

Freshly ground black pepper

1 Line a 25cm (10in) round cake tin or air fryer baskets with parchment paper. Brush the prepared tin or baskets with a little oil and scatter with the polenta or semolina. Set aside.

2 Put the flour and salt in a large bowl, mix together, then add the yeast and mix again. Add the tepid water gradually (you may not need it all) and 2 teaspoons of the oil. Mix with your hands until a slightly sticky dough forms. Tip onto a lightly floured work surface and knead for 10–12 minutes until the dough feels smooth and elastic. If using a stand mixer fitted with a dough hook attachment, knead for 5–6 minutes.

3 Place the dough in an oiled bowl and leave to prove in a warm place for 1–2 hours, or until roughly doubled in size. You can also refrigerate it overnight – just bring it up to room temperature before shaping.

4 Dust the work surface with flour and polenta (add more if it begins to stick) and tip the dough on top. Roll and stretch the dough into a 45x35cm (18x14in) rectangle.

5 Spread the pizza sauce on top, then scatter over both cheeses, the basil, if using, pizza herbs and a good grinding of black pepper. Tightly roll up the dough into a long sausage shape. Use a sharp knife to cut it into 9–10 pieces, and arrange cut-side up in the tin or baskets. Cover loosely with a tea towel and leave to prove for a further 30–45 minutes until the wheels look light and puffy.

6 Preheat the air fryer to 170°C. Bake for 20–25 minutes until golden brown and the cheese is oozing. Flip over to bake the undersides for the last 2 minutes, then turn back over and bake for a further minute. Cool for 5 minutes before serving. These pinwheels are best eaten within 24 hours.

Adaptations

(PB) *Substitute the mozzarella for vegan cheese, and use 1 tablespoon of nutritional yeast in place of the Parmesan.*

Fast forward

Cheat it with shop-bought pizza dough!

BREADGEHOG ROLLS

Kids and adults alike will love these little fellas with their crispy prickles! Stuff them with your favourite sandwich fillings or serve them with soup or a salad. They are so quick and easy to make with no second prove needed, but your friends will think you've spent hours making them! They don't hibernate, so you can have them all year round.

MAKES 10 ROLLS

PREP: 20–30
MINUTES
BAKE: 15–20
MINUTES

250g strong white
bread flour, plus
extra for dusting

250g multi-seed
or wholemeal
bread flour

10g fine sea salt

7g sachet fast-
action dried yeast

25g olive oil (or any
oil, or melted butter/
vegan spread), plus
extra for greasing

300g warm water

1 medium egg,
beaten, to glaze

A few black olives

1   Line two baking trays with parchment paper, or use silicone liners.

2   In a large bowl, mix both flours and salt, then add the yeast and mix through. Make a well in the centre and pour in the oil and warm water. Bring together with your hand, using your fingers in a claw shape to drag through the mixture until you have a dough. If the dough looks a little dry, add a few drops of water, but make sure the dough doesn't become too wet. Transfer to a work surface and pound, stretch and tear the dough and work the dough hard for 10–15 minutes until springy and bouncy.

3   If using a stand mixer fitted with a dough hook attachment, mix on slow until the dough comes together, then increase the speed to medium–high and knead for 5–7 minutes until very springy and bouncy.

4   Divide the dough in half, then divide each half into 5 equal size pieces. Dust the work surface with a little flour and roll each piece into a ball. To create a teardrop shape for the hedgehog, press the roll on one side and mould it into a point for the nose. Repeat with the remaining balls. Place on the prepared trays, leaving plenty of space between each piece as they will double in size. Cover loosely with oiled clingfilm or a damp tea towel. They will rise in about 1 hour, depending on the yeast and room temperature.

5   Using kitchen scissors or small craft scissors, carefully snip into the dough to create spikes, leaving the faces unsnipped, and work towards their bottoms. Brush with egg wash, then push in small pieces of olive for the eyes and nose.

6   Preheat the air fryer to 160°C. Bake for 15–20 minutes, then remove the paper and bake the undersides for a few more minutes, turning over to crisp off the bottoms if needed, until golden brown and cooked through. Leave to cool for 15 minutes.

7   If well wrapped, the rolls will keep for 2 days, or they can be frozen for up to a month.

CINNAMON BUNS

These bouncy, squishy cinnamon buns are the ultimate comfort feel-good food! Get them nestled into the baking tray the night before you wish to bake them so all you need to do is pop them in the air fryer for a perfect treat! These ones are cut to a slightly shorter depth than regular oven cinnamon buns, as they cook better this way when air fried.

MAKES 9 BUNS
PREP: 30 MINUTES
BAKE: 20–25 MINUTES

For the dough

115g milk

65g butter, melted

50g golden caster sugar

300g strong bread flour, plus extra for dusting

2 tsp ground cinnamon

½ tsp sea salt

7g sachet fast-action dried yeast

1 tsp vanilla extract

1 medium egg at room temperature

For the filling

75g unsalted butter, softened

90g light muscovado sugar

1 tsp ground cinnamon

1 medium egg, beaten, to glaze

Golden caster or brown sugar, for sprinkling

1   Line a 25cm (10in) square baking tray or dish with parchment paper, or if your air fryer drawer is of about this size, the buns can go directly in the basket.

2   Start by making the dough. Heat the milk in a small saucepan until warm. In a separate pan, melt the butter.

3   Put all the dry ingredients in the bowl of a stand mixer fitted with a dough hook attachment (ensuring you put the salt and yeast onto separate sides of the bowl) and give a little mix to combine.

4   Combine the warmed milk, melted butter, vanilla and egg and mix together. Pour into the dry ingredients.

5   Knead on slow to begin with until the dough comes together, then increase the speed to medium–high and knead for 5–6 minutes until the dough is very springy and pliable. The dough should be smooth and only slightly tacky to the touch. If it is still too sticky, add 1–2 tablespoons of extra flour. Alternatively, knead by hand vigorously for 10–12 minutes.

6   Grease a large bowl and place the dough inside. Cover with a damp, warm tea towel and leave to prove for about 1 hour until doubled in size.

7   Meanwhile, make the filling. Cream the butter, muscovado sugar and cinnamon together until pale and creamy – this can be done by hand or in the stand mixer.

8   Sprinkle a large area of work surface with flour. Roll the dough out into a 35x25cm (14x10in) rectangle about 7mm (¼in) thick. Spread the filling all over the dough using a palette knife. Roll up the dough and cut it into nine rolls – it's a good idea to measure the dough and cut it into three lengths, then cut each length into three again to keep the rolls roughly equal in size.

recipe continued overleaf . . .

For the cream cheese icing (optional)

50g full-fat cream cheese, at room temperature

15g unsalted butter, very soft

75g icing sugar, sifted

½ tsp vanilla extract or bean paste

9   Place the rolls on the prepared tray in three rows of three, and space them out evenly. They will puff up and touch each other once risen. They can also be frozen at this point for air frying at a later stage. Cover and leave to rise for about 45 minutes–1 hour until a little expanded and puffy. Brush the rolls with egg wash and sprinkle with caster sugar.

10 Preheat the air fryer to 170°C. Bake for 20–25 minutes until golden brown. Check the undersides; if they are a little doughy you can carefully flip these over (wear oven gloves and use a large slice to aid flipping). Bake for a few more minutes until the base is crisp and turning darker, then turn over the right way again and bake for a further minute. Leave to cool in the tray for 5 minutes.

11 Meanwhile, make the cream cheese icing. Mash the cream cheese and butter together, then beat in the icing sugar and vanilla until smooth. Spread generously over the cooled buns, or leave them plain, if you prefer.

12 Un-iced buns will keep for a day and can be microwaved briefly to warm, or refreshed in the air fryer at 140°C for a few minutes.

Adaptation

(DF) *Substitute the butter for vegan block butter or spread.*

TIPS

• *Use dental floss to get a really neat finish when cutting the buns without squishing them.*

• *You can freeze some or all of the rolls once you have rolled them up and before their second prove.*

• *Bake in smaller batches of 3–4 if you have a smaller air fryer basket.*

CLASSIC CHOCOLATE-GLAZED DOUGHNUTS

There's no denying the worldwide love for these sugary round confections. Just ask Homer Simpson! All the fun of the fair but without the deep frying. No greasy fingers with these beauties. Sugary yes, but slightly less guilt inducing. These are best eaten freshly baked and still warm.

MAKES 8–10 DOUGHNUTS

PREP: 20 MINUTES
BAKE: 8 MINUTES

For the dough

250g white bread flour, plus extra for dusting

30g caster sugar

¼ tsp sea salt

7g sachet fast-action dried yeast

60g unsalted butter, softened

1 medium egg

1 tsp vanilla extract or bean paste

110g whole milk, slightly warmed

Cooking spray and melted butter, to grease and brush

For the chocolate glaze

50g butter

25g golden syrup or honey

150g plain chocolate chips or chopped chocolate

1   Line two baking trays with parchment paper, or use silicone liners.

2   Start by making the dough. In a stand mixer fitted with a dough hook attachment, combine the flour, sugar and salt, then add the yeast and mix to distribute. Add the butter, egg, vanilla and warm milk and bring together on a low speed into a shaggy dough. Increase the speed to medium and knead for 4–5 minutes until the dough feels smooth and springy. (Add extra flour if the dough feels too sticky. It needs to be a little sticky but come together well once kneaded.)

3   Alternatively, you can do this by hand in a large bowl, bringing the ingredients together with your hand in a claw until the dough is shaggy, then tip it onto a work surface and knead for 10–15 minutes to a smooth, springy ball.

4   Transfer the dough to a lightly oiled bowl and cover with oiled clingfilm or a damp tea towel. Leave in a warm place for 45 minutes–2 hours until almost doubled in size. The timing will depend on the yeast and the room temperature.

5   Tip the dough out and knead a little by hand to knock it back, then lightly dust the surface with flour and roll the dough out to about 1.5cm (¾in) thick. Cut out circles using a 6.5cm (2½in) cutter, then cut a smaller circle in the centre of the large circle for the hole using a 2cm (¾in) cutter. Reroll the scraps to use up all the dough.

6   Place the circles on the prepared baking trays or directly in lined baskets, making sure to leave plenty of room between each as they will puff up when rising and during the bake. Once risen, they are delicate, so it's best not to move or handle them too much.

recipe continued overleaf . . .

7 Cover loosely with lightly oiled clingfilm and leave for 30–40 minutes until almost doubled in size, or you can put them in the fridge overnight to prove slowly, bringing them back up to room temperature the following day and allowing them to puff up before air frying.

8 Preheat the air fryer to 180°C. Brush the doughnuts with a little oil or melted butter. Bake for 6–8 minutes. The first couple you bake will give you an indication of how long they need to bake for, as all air fryers vary. Turn them over to bake evenly.

9 Meanwhile, make the chocolate glaze. Very gently heat all the ingredients together in a small saucepan, stirring until you get a shiny, smooth mixture.

10 Have a wire rack ready, with a sheet of parchment paper underneath to catch the drips. Put the glaze in a shallow bowl wide enough to accommodate the doughnuts. Using either your fingers or a couple of forks, dip each doughnut just over halfway into the glaze, holding it flat, to glaze the top. Turn them over and place on the wire rack. Leave to set (or for as long as you can resist) before devouring!

ICED BUNS

These take me back to when I was little, walking to the Home Made Bakery in Leigh-on-Sea after school, where their iced buns were always pink or white. I always bought pink ones! We used to have them once a week as a special treat, along with doughnut men or gingerbread men (but not all at the same time). I taught Dermot O'Leary how to make these for *Bake Off*, and of course he was crowned Star Baker!

MAKES 8 BUNS

PREP: 25 MINUTES

BAKE: 12 MINUTES

For the dough

125g milk

25g butter, softened

275g strong white bread flour, plus extra for dusting

15g caster sugar

7g sachet fast-action dried yeast

1 tsp sea salt

1 medium egg, beaten

Oil, for greasing

For the icing

250g fondant sugar icing (you can use regular icing sugar, but it will set sticky)

A couple of drops of food colouring (optional)

1   Line a baking tray with parchment paper, or use a silicone liner.

2   Start by making the dough. Heat the milk and butter in a saucepan until lukewarm.

3   Put all the dry ingredients into the bowl of a stand mixer fitted with a dough hook attachment (or work by hand). Add the yeast to one side of the bowl and the salt to the other to avoid killing the yeast. Add the warmed milk mixture and beaten egg and mix on a high speed for 8 minutes until the dough is smooth and elastic. All flours vary in absorbency, so if you need a little more liquid, add a dash more milk. Place the dough in an oiled bowl and leave to prove for 45 minutes, or until doubled in size. The timing will depend on the yeast and the room temperature.

4   Turn the dough out onto a lightly floured work surface and knock it back by kneading it for about 1 minute until smooth. It helps to rub your hands with a little sunflower or light olive oil before handling the dough to avoid sticking and using too much extra flour, which can dry out the dough.

5   Divide the dough into 8 equal pieces. Roll into balls first, then into 10–12cm (4–5in) long fingers. Try to get them all a similar size.

6   Place the fingers in a line onto the prepared baking tray, leaving 2cm (¾in) between each so that they just touch each other when risen. If you have a smaller air fryer you may only be able to put two fingers into a basket, so pop them in pairs onto parchment paper or into silicone dishes to rise, so that you can drop them directly into the air fryer without having to lift them up and spoil the rise. If you need to, refrigerate the fingers to slow down the rise. Cover loosely with oiled clingfilm and leave in a warm place to prove for 30 minutes.

7   Preheat the air fryer to 180°C. Bake for 7–8 minutes, then remove the parchment paper and bake for a further 2–3 minutes directly on the vented tray or basket to crisp off the bases. If the bottoms feel a little soggy, turn the fingers over for the last minute to dry them out, then transfer to a wire rack to cool completely.

8   Meanwhile, make the icing. Mix the icing sugar with 2–3 teaspoons of water, adding the water a drop at a time so that the icing is runny enough to dip into but still hold its shape atop each bun without running off. Colour the icing, if you wish.

9   To ice, turn each bun upside down and push into the icing to cover in a line on the top, lift up and remove any excess with a damp finger. Turn over and set onto a wire rack to set. They shouldn't be drippy, the icing should stay in a neat line on the top of each pillowy bun.

SEASONAL & CELEBRATIONS

CHRISTMAS CAKE

Wait – you can bake a Christmas cake in an air fryer?, I hear you cry! Indeed you can. Yes, I know, it's a Christmas miracle. Christmas for us just isn't Christmas without this cake. This recipe is the one I baked for Fortnum & Mason for many years. I believe it's the world's best fruitcake, and now you can air fry it, too!

MAKES 20CM (8IN) ROUND CAKE OR 15CM (6IN) 2-LAYER ROUND CAKES (SERVES 10–12)

PREP: 20 MINUTES

BAKE: 2 HOURS FOR 15CM (6IN), 2½ HOURS FOR 20CM (8IN)

240g sultanas

360g raisins

360g currants

100g mixed peel

300g natural-colour glacé cherries, rinsed and halved

60g glacé ginger or stem ginger, finely chopped

200g salted butter

200g molasses sugar

4 medium eggs

2 tsp vanilla extract

220g plain flour

½ tsp ground cinnamon

½ tsp ground ginger

¼ tsp ground nutmeg

½ tsp mixed spice

Pinch of ground cloves

160g (6–8 tbsp) brandy, plus extra 100g to feed

70g vodka

1 Grease and line a 7.5cm (3in) deep 20cm (8in) round solid-base cake tin, or two 15cm (6in) tins of the same depth.

2 Put the dried fruit, cherries and glacé ginger in a bowl large enough to hold the whole mixture and mix together with a large wooden spoon.

3 Put the butter and sugar in a small, microwave-safe bowl and heat in 1-minute bursts, stirring with a whisk between each burst. If you don't have a microwave, do this in a non-stick pan over a low heat.

4 In a small bowl, beat the eggs and vanilla together.

5 In another bowl, mix the flour and spices together. Add the spiced flour to the fruit and mix with your hands. Tip the melted butter and sugar mixture into the large bowl of fruit and flour and mix well. Add the beaten eggs and mix well. Finally, add the brandy and vodka.

6 Preheat the air fryer to 140°C. Bake for 1 hour, then decrease the heat to 125°C and bake for about 1½ hours for the larger cake or 1 hour for the two smaller cakes until completely cooked through. A skewer inserted into the centre should come out almost clean.

7 While still hot and still in the tin(s), spike the cake(s) all over with a skewer and pour over more brandy to soak the cake. Let cool.

8 Remove from the tin(s) once cool, double wrap in parchment paper, then wrap in strong foil. The cake can be eaten after a week, but ideally make this a few weeks before you need it. You can even store it for up to a year in a cool, dry place, feeding with extra brandy if you wish every so often.

Adaptations

(DF) *Substitute the butter for vegan block butter.*

(GF) *Substitute the flour for a gluten-free blend.*

(PB) *Make the dairy-free substitutions. Substitute the eggs for 4 x flax eggs, see Tip on p83.*

CHRISTMAS PUDDING COOKIES

A plethora of festive flavours in handy cookie form! Santa won't be able to resist them, nor will the elves, the reindeer or even Scrooge. These little puds are lovely for festive gatherings and also make really lovely edible Christmas gifts if you wrap them up in gift bags and tie them with ribbon.

MAKES 8 COOKIES
PREP: 20 MINUTES
BAKE: 22 MINUTES

50g butter

1 tbsp treacle

1 medium egg

215g plain flour

1½ tsp ground ginger

25g glacé or stem ginger, chopped

½ tsp bicarbonate of soda

50g light muscovado sugar

50g golden caster sugar

To decorate

100g white chocolate, melted

Sprinkles of your choice for the holly and berries, or green and red writing icing

1 Line a baking tray with parchment paper, or use a silicone liner.

2 Gently heat the butter and treacle in a small saucepan, stirring until melted. Set aside to cool slightly. Beat in the egg and set aside.

3 Put the flour, ground ginger, glacé or stem ginger, bicarbonate of soda and both sugars in a mixing bowl. Mix well, then stir in the wet ingredients. Bring the mixture together to form a dough.

4 Divide the dough into 8 equal pieces and roll into balls. Place on the prepared baking tray and flatten to about 1cm (½in) thick. If you're making these in batches, pop them in the fridge on a paper-lined tray to firm up so you can drop them into the air fryer baskets after the first lot are baked.

5 Preheat the air fryer to 140°C. Bake for 18–22 minutes, or until golden and firm around the edges. Leave to firm up on the trays or in the baskets for a few minutes, then transfer to a wire rack to cool completely.

6 To decorate, dip the biscuits in the melted chocolate and use a spoon to push the chocolate up the biscuits in a wavy line so it looks like a pudding drip. Place on a baking tray lined with parchment paper to set and scatter over sprinkles to create a holly and berry effect. Alternatively, use some green and red icing to pipe on the design.

ELF SPAGHETTI CUPCAKES

Elf is one of my favourite holiday movies, and these themed cupcakes look so effective but are actually really easy to make, unless you're a Cotton-headed Ninny Muggins! You don't even need any special equipment as you can use a food bag or parchment paper cone to pipe the buttercream spaghetti.

MAKES ABOUT 12 CUPCAKES

PREP: 20 MINUTES
BAKE: 15 MINUTES

For the sponge

150g butter, softened

120g golden caster sugar

30g pure maple syrup

3 medium eggs

150g self-raising flour

½ tsp baking powder

1 tsp ground cinnamon

For the buttercream

150g butter, softened

300g icing sugar

1 tsp vanilla bean paste

Caramel/yellow food colouring

To decorate

A handful of Frosted Shreddies

Smarties (red and green)

White mini marshmallows

Christmas-themed sprinkles

1 tbsp maple syrup, for drizzling

1   Line two six-hole cupcake tins with paper cases, or use individual silicone moulds.

2   Start by making the sponge. Beat the butter, sugar and maple syrup together until pale and creamy. Add the eggs one at a time, beating well after each addition. Stir in the flour, baking powder and cinnamon. Divide the mixture equally between the cases.

3   Preheat the air fryer to 150°C. Bake for 12–15 minutes. Turn the cupcakes over and bake for a further 2 minutes if the bottoms feel a bit soggy. Remove from the air fryer and transfer onto a wire rack to cool completely.

4   Meanwhile, make the buttercream. Beat the butter, icing sugar and vanilla together until pale and fluffy. Colour to the desired shade of spaghetti yellow and put into a piping bag or food bag. Snip a 3mm hole in the bag and pipe wiggly spaghetti all over the cupcakes. Dress with the Elf-themed decorations, adding a small drizzle of maple syrup over the top.

TIP
For the Christmas-themed sprinkles, I used an Off Piste mix from Truly Sprinkles.

CANDY CANE FOREST SHOWSTOPPER CHRISTMAS CAKE

This is my homage to Williams Sonoma, the US cookware retailer, which is one of my favourite places to shop. I'm obsessed! This is a bit of a project but well worth it. It looks so cool when you cut into it, but it's not as technical as you'd think. All you need are piping bags or food bags to pipe the white and red icings in rings. This cake is a great one to make because you can bake the sponges up to a week ahead and get the frostings ready. The decorating time isn't as long as you'd think, and if you want to simplify, you can just add fluffy flicky-style frosting and adorn the cake with red and white sprinkles and some candy canes.

MAKES 15CM (6IN) 3-LAYER ROUND CAKE (SERVES 12–14)

PREP: 1½ HOURS

CHILL: 30 MINUTES

BAKE: 22 MINUTES

For the sponge

200g salted butter, softened

280g light muscovado sugar

4 medium eggs, beaten

160g plain chocolate chips, melted and cooled slightly

1–2 tsp peppermint extract, to taste (I used Nielsen Massey)

160g plain flour

For the frosting

350g white chocolate, melted then cooled

500g unsalted butter, softened

1 Line three 15cm (6in) round cake tins with parchment paper, or use silicone moulds.

2 Start by making the sponge. Using a stand mixer or electric hand mixer, cream the butter and sugar on high until pale and fluffy, or cream by hand with a wooden spoon. Reduce the speed to low and add the beaten eggs a little at a time until incorporated. Pour in the chocolate, beating all the time, then stir in the peppermint extract. Fold in the flour until just incorporated. Divide equally between the prepared tins and level off.

3 Preheat the air fryer to 140°C. Bake for 18–22 minutes until just cooked (do this in batches if you have a small air fryer). The cakes should be well risen but still wobble a little when shaken, and a skewer inserted into the centre should come out a little pasty, not glistening and wet, but not dry. These cakes are more like brownies, so will have a crust on the top. The crust will sink back into the cake as it cools. Leave to cool in the tins for 10–15 minutes, then carefully turn out onto a wire rack to cool completely.

4 To make the icing, gently melt the chocolate until smooth and lump free, then set aside to cool slightly but not set.

5 Beat the butter and peppermint extract until very pale and creamy, then add half the icing sugar, beating slowly until the sugar is incorporated, then increase the speed and beat well until very light and fluffy. Repeat with the second half of the icing sugar.

recipe continued overleaf . . .

1–2 tsp peppermint extract, to taste (I used Nielsen Massey)

750g icing sugar

2–3 tbsp milk, to loosen

Bright-red food colouring gel (I used Rainbow Dust Red)

To decorate

100–150 Christmas-theme sprinkles (I used a selection of red and white ones from Truly Sprinkles, including red macaroni rods)

Candy canes and peppermint sweets, to decorate

6 Add the cooled melted white chocolate to the mix and beat in well until fully incorporated and light and fluffy. Lastly, add a little milk to loosen. You want the icing to hold its shape but be soft and spreadable.

7 To make the stripy filling, weigh 300g of frosting and colour it red, then transfer it to a piping bag. Put another 300g of white frosting into a separate piping bag.

8 If the cakes need levelling, you can trim the tops a little, but they usually come out quite flat.

9 To assemble, secure one of the cakes, crust-side up, to a 15cm (6in) cake drum with a little frosting. Fix the drum onto a larger 25cm (10in) board by securing with more frosting. Snip a hole in both piping bags and pipe a 5mm (¼in) thick white ring around the edge of the cake.

10 Now pipe a ring of red icing inside the outer circle, and continue alternating between the white and red icings. Top with the second cake, crust-side up, and repeat the stripy icing.

11 Invert the last sponge so that the crust faces down and press it onto the cakes. Go around the cakes with the white icing to crumb coat it. Chill for at least 30 minutes before adding the rest of the white icing to coat the cake as neatly as possible, using a palette knife and a side smoother. Using the flat of your hand, press a band of sprinkles around the base of the cake and place any larger sprinkles or rods as you wish, taking care not to damage the icing. Add the candy canes and sweets.

12 This cake keeps for up to a week or can be frozen.

Adaptations

(DF) *Substitute the butter for vegan block butter or spread and use dairy-free chocolate and plant milk.*

(GF) *Substitute the flour for a gluten-free blend.*

MINCE PIES

Christmas wouldn't be Christmas without these little guys. Home-baked mince pies are always so much better, but I don't bother making the mincemeat from scratch. I use shop-bought mincemeat and add extra oomph with orange zest and a splash of booze. Using homemade pastry and baking them fresh is wonderful as the smell of Christmas will emanate from your air fryer! If you haven't tried it already, my favourite way to eat them is sliced in half through the middle with a wedge of Lancashire cheese slotted in.

**MAKES 12
MINCE PIES**

PREP: 30 MINUTES

CHILL: 30 MINUTES

BAKE: 17 MINUTES

For the mincemeat

400g shop-bought mincemeat

Zest of 1 or 2 oranges, to taste

20g Courvoisier or alcohol of choice

For the pastry

250g plain flour, plus extra for dusting

40g icing sugar

Pinch of sea salt

125g unsalted butter, chilled and cubed

1 medium egg, plus 1 yolk

1 medium egg, beaten, to glaze

Granulated sugar, for sprinkling

A little melted butter

1 Brush 12 foil pie cases with melted butter and refrigerate, or grease cupcake tins if you have a larger air fryer.

2 Tip the mincemeat into a bowl and stir in the orange zest and Courvoisier (this will make a little more filling than you need for one batch – as a guide you will need 40–45g per pie). Set aside.

3 To make the pastry, put the flour, icing sugar and salt in a food processor. Blitz to mix, then add the butter and blitz again until the mixture resembles breadcrumbs. Add the egg and yolk and blitz for a further 45 seconds–1 minute until the mixture comes together and forms clumps of dough. Tip out onto a lightly floured work surface and bring together into a ball, then flatten out. Roll out the dough to a 2mm thickness. Use a round cutter to cut 12 circles large enough to line the base and side of the cases. Cut 12 smaller circles that will cover the pies. Line the refrigerated moulds with the larger circles, pushing down neatly with your fingertips.

4 Fill the pastry cases almost to the top with mincemeat. Brush around the edges with egg wash and press the pastry lids firmly onto the base to seal. Poke small holes into the lids for the steam to escape. Reroll any pastry scraps and cut out Christmas shapes to decorate.

5 Refrigerate for 30 minutes, or freeze until needed. When ready to bake, brush with egg wash and sprinkle with sugar.

6 Preheat the air fryer to 180°C. Bake for 15–17 minutes until golden and crisp. If baking from frozen, the pies will need a few extra minutes. Leave to cool in the cases for about 15 minutes, then carefully release and lift out with a knife. Serve warm or at room temperature.

Adaptations

(DF) *Substitute the butter for vegan block butter or spread.*

(GF) *Substitute the flour for a gluten-free blend.*

GINGERBREAD LATTE CUPCAKES

These cupcakes look adorable with little marzipan cut-outs of mini gingerbread men. If you don't like marzipan, use modelling chocolate or sugar paste instead. Alternatively just add some gold and rose gold sprinkles for decoration. The food colours I have used to get the gingerbread shade are Paprika Flesh and Chocolate Brown, both by Sugarflair. It is quite an orangey brown, but feel free to use any colourings you have to hand. All ingredients should be at room temperature.

MAKES 12 CUPCAKES
PREP: 30 MINUTES
BAKE: 18 MINUTES

For the gingerbread-style decorations (optional)

100g marzipan, modelling chocolate or sugar paste

1–2 drops of colouring of choice

Icing sugar, for dusting

For the icing on the gingerbread decorations

2 tbsp soft peak white royal icing (see p53)

For the sponge

200g self-raising flour

½ tsp baking powder

2 tsp ground ginger

1 tsp ground cinnamon

120g unsalted butter, diced and softened

150g light muscovado or soft brown sugar

20g black treacle

90g stem ginger in syrup from a jar, blitzed

2 medium eggs

200g buttermilk

1   Make the gingerbread-style decorations in advance, if using. To colour the marzipan, add a couple of tiny dots of gel paste colour to it using the end of a sharp knife, as colours can be really strong, you can add more until you reach the desired shade. Knead for 1–2 minutes so it becomes smooth and pliable and the colour is fully mixed in. Roll out to a 3–4mm (¼in) thickness and cut out little gingerbread men shapes using a mini cookie cutter. Pop onto a board dusted with icing sugar to dry.

2   Using a couple of tablespoons of soft peak royal icing in a piping bag fitted with a No. 1.5 round nozzle (or cut a 1.5mm hole in the bag), pipe little faces and details such as buttons, to bring the gingerbread men to life. Set aside to dry. If you're short on time, use shop-bought mini gingerbread biscuit men or just crumble ginger biscuits on top, or add jolly festive metallic sprinkles.

3   Line two six-hole cupcake tins with paper cases, or use individual silicone moulds.

4   To make the sponge, sift or whisk together the flour, baking powder and spices together.

5   In a separate bowl, cream the butter, sugar, treacle and stem ginger on medium speed for a few minutes until pale and fluffy. Add the eggs one at a time, beating well after each addition. Add the flour and buttermilk in three batches (flour then buttermilk) until all mixed in. Divide the batter equally between the cupcake cases.

6   Preheat the air fryer to 150°C. Bake for 15–18 minutes, or until risen, springy and a skewer inserted into the centre comes out clean. Turn over and bake upside-down for a further 2 minutes if needed to ensure the bottoms are completely cooked. Leave to cool in the tin, then pierce all over with a skewer (this will help to soak up the coffee syrup).

For the coffee syrup

About 20g good-quality instant espresso powder, to taste

70g caster sugar

80g boiling water

Shot of coffee liqueur (optional)

For the icing

200g unsalted butter, softened

100g full-fat cream cheese, at room temperature

400g unrefined icing sugar, sifted (regular is also fine)

7   To make the coffee syrup, mix the coffee, sugar and boiling water together and stir until dissolved. Add the coffee liqueur, if using. Drizzle or brush the coffee syrup evenly over the cakes. Leave to cool completely on a wire rack.

8   For the icing, cream the butter and cream cheese together until soft and creamy. Add the icing sugar, one-quarter at a time, and whisk on a low speed. When all the icing sugar has been added, increase the speed to high for 1 minute to make the icing very light.

9   Put the icing into a piping bag fitted with a 1cm round or star nozzle, or just snip the end of the bag. If you don't wish to do any piping, spread some buttercream over the cupcakes using a small cranked palette knife or regular knife and make a flicky swoosh on the top. Garnish with the gingerbread decorations or simply crumble some shop-bought ginger biscuits over the top or use metallic sprinkles.

HOMEMADE BUTTERMILK

If you can't get hold of buttermilk you can easily make your own. Sour 200g of whole milk by adding 2 teaspoons of apple cider vinegar or lemon juice to it. It's that simple! Alternatively, use half natural yoghurt and half milk – stir together and leave to sour.

CINNAMON SPICED TAHINI XMAS CAKE

This cake is bursting with spicy cinnamon for that festive feel. This recipe includes tahini, which isn't necessarily the first thing you think of when making a Christmas cake, but the toasted sesame flavour actually complements the other ingredients perfectly. In fact, it will make you feel all warm and toasty! Finished off with a golden Biscoff drip and a delicate sugared rosemary wreath, this one is guaranteed to steal the show!

MAKES 20CM (8IN) 2-LAYER ROUND CAKE (SERVES 12–14)

PREP: 1 HOUR 15 MINUTES

BAKE: 22 MINUTES

For the sponge

150g softened butter

50g tahini (well stirred)

100g golden caster sugar

100g light muscovado sugar

4 medium eggs

225g self-raising flour

2 tsp ground cinnamon

½ tsp ground ginger

2–3 Tbsp milk

For the buttercream

250g unsalted butter, softened

2 tsp ground cinnamon

50g tahini (well stirred)

500g icing sugar, sifted

1 Tbsp treacle

1 Grease and line two 20cm (8in) round tins, or use silicone moulds.

2 Start by making the sugared rosemary. It's best to make this the day before so it can dry. Beat the egg white until foamy and brush it over the rosemary sprigs with a pastry brush so that they are sticky but not wet. Dredge in the sugar and set aside to dry on a piece of baking paper. (You can speed up the drying in the air fryer; just place the sprigs onto the racks or in the basket and heat on 100°C for about 1 hour.)

3 To make the sponge, cream the butter, tahini and both sugars until pale, fluffy and creamy. Add the eggs one at a time, beating well after each addition.

4 In a separate bowl, dry-whisk the flour with the spices, or mix with a fork. Fold the flour into the wet ingredients until incorporated, then add the milk to loosen the batter. Divide the batter equally between the prepared tins and level the surface with a spoon or palette knife.

5 Preheat the air fryer to 150°C. Bake for 18–22 minutes, or until springy, golden and risen. A skewer inserted into the centre of the cakes should come out clean. Leave to cool in the tins for 5 minutes, then turn out onto a wire rack to cool completely, removing the paper.

6 Meanwhile, whip up the buttercream. Beat the butter, cinnamon, tahini and sugar until pale, smooth and creamy. Beat in the treacle.

recipe continued overleaf . . .

A little egg white

Some fresh rosemary sprigs

50g caster sugar

To decorate

75g Biscoff spread

Gold sprinkles

Gold lustre

Star anise

White chocolate balls (I used Lindor)

7   Trim the tops of the cakes to make them level, if necessary. Place a cake on a plate or stand and spread generously with about 350g of the buttercream, allowing it to come right to the edge. Place the second cake upside-down over the buttercream, so that the smooth bottom is now the top. Smooth around the join and spread a thin layer of buttercream over the whole cake to seal in the crumbs. Refrigerate for about 30 minutes.

8   Spread over the remaining buttercream to get a neat finish on the top and sides. Refrigerate for another 30 minutes–1 hour.

9   Stand a jar of Biscoff in some hot water, or spoon out the required amount into a microwave-safe dish and gently heat until a little runny. Pipe or spoon this around the top edge of the cake to create a pretty drip effect. If piping, hold the bag up against the top edge of the cake and create a pool of Biscoff around the edge, allowing some of the Biscoff to drip down the sides. Using a piping bag allows you to better control the Biscoff and achieve neater thin lines, but of course you can use a spoon for more freestyle drips.

10 Dress the cake with a ring of sugared rosemary: position sprigs of rosemary around the edge of the cake to form a circle. Accessorise the drips with a few gold sprinkles. Top lustred star anise and chocolate balls to create a pretty wreath design.

11 Best served at room temperature. Wrapped, the cake will keep for up to 3 days, or for up to a week if refrigerated. It can also be frozen for up to 3 months.

LEFTOVER CHEESEBOARD STRAWS

If you're anything like me at Christmas and New Year, my eyes are too big for my belly and I always buy too much cheese! These biscuits are great to use up any leftover hard fatty cheeses like Black Bomber, our family favourite, or blue cheeses like Stilton, Blacksticks Blue or Stichelton (use a mix if you like). They make the most perfect delicate cheese straws – great for New Year nibbles!

MAKES 15–20 STRAWS

PREP: 10 MINUTES

CHILL: 1 HOUR

BAKE: 12 MINUTES

175g plain flour

150g butter, chilled and cubed

150g mix of strong hard cheese, such as Cheddar or Stilton, crumbled or grated

1 Line a baking sheet with parchment paper, or use a silicone liner.

2 Whizz all the ingredients together in a bowl with 1–2 tablespoons of cold water to make a dough. Chill for 30 minutes if it's too soft to work with.

3 Roll out between two pieces of parchment paper to a 3–4mm thickness. Cut into strips or star shapes using a pastry cutter, then transfer to the prepared baking sheet. Chill for at least 30 minutes.

4 Preheat the air fryer to 180°C. Bake for 8–12 minutes until light golden and the straws look like they're drying out and crisp. Turn over to crisp off the bottoms for the last 2 minutes, if needed.

5 Cool for a few minutes on the baking sheet. They will keep for 5 days in an airtight container – not that they will last that long!

CHOCOLATE ORANGE CUPCAKES

These divine cupcakes are decadent, dark and fudgy – perfect for winter gatherings or as a great alternative to a traditional Christmas cake. They look very impressive with a shimmering chocolate or candied orange slice, which you can buy online or make yourself. Serve as they come or as a dessert alongside whipped cream or crème fraîche. If you prefer, chocolate orange segments also work really well with these in place of the candied orange.

MAKES 12 CUPCAKES
PREP: 30 MINUTES
BAKE: 14 MINUTES

For the sponge

150g salted butter, softened

150g plain chocolate, chopped

180g light muscovado sugar

Zest of 1 large orange

3 medium eggs, plus 1 yolk

1 tsp vanilla extract

125g soured cream, at room temperature

140g self-raising flour

30g cocoa powder

For the buttercream

250g unsalted butter, softened

500g icing sugar, sifted

190g plain chocolate, melted and cooled

Zest of 1 orange

A little milk, to loosen

1 Line two six-hole cupcake tins with paper cases, or use individual silicone moulds.

2 Start by making the sponge. Gently melt the butter, chocolate and sugar in the microwave in 30-second bursts, stirring between bursts so it doesn't catch. Alternatively, you can melt the ingredients in a large bowl set over a pan of simmering water until the chocolate chips have melted to a smooth liquid. Remove from the heat and leave to cool a little, then stir in the orange zest.

3 In a separate bowl, beat the eggs, vanilla and soured cream together.

4 Sift the flour and cocoa powder into another bowl and mix to combine. Stir the egg mixture into the cooled chocolate, then fold through the flour mix. Divide the batter equally between the cases, filling them three-quarters full.

5 Preheat the air fryer to 150°C. Bake for 12–14 minutes. They should be still wobbly inside and a skewer inserted into the centre should come out a little fudgy. Allow the cakes to cool in the tin for 10 minutes, then transfer to a wire rack to cool completely.

6 While the cakes are baking, make the buttercream. Beat the butter until pale and creamy. Gradually add the icing sugar, beating well after each addition.

7 Melt the chocolate in the microwave in 30-second bursts, stirring between each burst to ensure it doesn't catch. Let it cool slightly, then mix it through the buttercream with the orange zest, adding a little milk if needed – the buttercream should be of a soft consistency that will hold its shape when piping.

recipe continued overleaf . . .

To decorate

A few slices of candied orange, dipped in melted chocolate (see box)

Edible gold lustre or spray (optional)

8 To decorate the cupcakes, swirl some buttercream over the top using a piping bag fitted with a star nozzle and plunge in a segment of chocolate orange or a candied orange slice. If you'd like to jazz it up a little, you can add a spray of gold lustre to make it shine!

9 The cupcakes will keep for up to 3 days and freeze well for up to a month.

Adaptation

(GF) *Substitute the flour for a gluten-free blend.*

CANDIED ORANGE SLICES

If you want to make your own candied orange slices, it's best to do this the day before, or this can be done in advance as they will keep well in an airtight container for up to a month.

300g golden caster sugar

2 oranges, cut into 3–4mm (¼in) thick slices

Put the sugar and 300g of water in a medium–large saucepan and bring to the boil, then reduce to a gentle simmer. Pop in the orange slices and simmer for about 1 hour until the pith turns translucent, turning occasionally. Line a baking tray with parchment paper. Carefully remove the slices from the syrup, shake off the excess liquid and place on the tray. Set aside to dry overnight. Once dry, you can dip them in chocolate, if you wish. To do this, melt 100g of plain chocolate in a small bowl. Dip each slice about halfway and set to dry on fresh parchment paper until set. Any left-over chocolate can be saved and used in the sponge recipe.

HOT CROSS BUNS

The quantities given here make twelve hot cross buns – perfect if you have a large family-size air fryer with multiple racks. Otherwise, halve the quantities to make six. Any leftover buns can be made into toasted cheese sandwiches (my favourite!) for that sweet and savoury combo (don't knock it till you've tried it!) or bread and butter pudding. Just use the recipe on p142 and swap the croissants for sliced hot cross buns. If it's Easter time, add any Easter chocolates you fancy!

MAKES 12 HOT CROSS BUNS
PREP: 30 MINUTES
BAKE: 20 MINUTES

For the dough

200g sultanas

100g boiling water

230g whole milk

50g butter

1 medium egg

500g strong white bread flour, plus extra for dusting

1 tsp sea salt

75g golden caster sugar

7g sachet fast-action dried yeast

2 tsp mixed spice powder

1 tsp ground cinnamon

1 tsp ground ginger

Finely grated zest of ½ lemon

Finely grated zest of ½ orange

50g mixed candied peel, finely chopped

25g glacé or stem ginger, chopped (optional)

Oil, for greasing

1 Line a couple of baking trays with parchment paper, or use silicone liners.

2 Start by making the dough. Soak the sultanas in the boiling water and set aside.

3 In a saucepan, heat the milk with the butter until lukewarm, then beat in the egg.

4 Put the flour, salt, sugar and yeast into a bowl. Make a well in the centre. Pour in the warm milk mixture and add the remaining ingredients. Using a wooden spoon, mix well, then bring everything together with your hands until you have a sticky dough.

5 Tip onto a lightly floured work surface and knead by holding the dough with one hand and stretching it with the heel of the other hand, then folding it back on itself. Repeat for 5 minutes until smooth and elastic. This can be done in a stand mixer fitted with a dough hook, if you have one.

6 Put the dough in a lightly oiled bowl. Cover with oiled clingfilm and leave to rise in a warm place for 1 hour, or until doubled in size and a finger pressed into it leaves a dent.

7 Divide the dough into 12 equal pieces. Roll each piece into a smooth ball.

8 Arrange the buns on the prepared trays, or into air fryer baskets lined with parchment paper, leaving enough space for the dough to expand. Cover (but don't wrap) with more oiled clingfilm, or a tea towel, then set aside to prove for 1 hour more, or until very puffy and risen and doubled in size (the buns should just touch each other).

recipe continued overleaf . . .

For the cross and glaze

75g plain flour

2 tbsp apricot jam

9   To make the cross, mix the flour with 2–3 tablespoons of cold water. Add the water 1 tablespoon at a time, adding just enough to make a thick paste. Spoon into a piping bag fitted with a small nozzle or cut a 5mm hole in the bag. Pipe a line along each row of buns, then repeat in the other direction to create crosses.

10   Preheat the air fryer to 160°C. Bake for 15–18 minutes. Make sure the bottoms are fully cooked – turn them over if needed – and bake for a further 2 minutes. Transfer to a wire rack to cool slightly.

11   Meanwhile, make the glaze by heating up the apricot jam with 2 teaspoons of water. Brush the warm jam over the top of the warm buns and leave to cool.

TIP
I like to rub a little neutral cooking oil into my hands when handling and shaping dough, rather than using too much more flour as it will make the dough drier. You can dust the surface with flour if you prefer, but I like to try not to use extra flour.

SPECKLED EGG CAKE

Discover your inner Jackson Pollock with this light and fluffy vanilla cake flicked with pastel speckled-egg icing and topped off with a tasty egg nest – so cute to make for Easter. This cake looks lovely in any pastel shade, so make it your own.

MAKES 15CM (6IN) 3-LAYER ROUND CAKE (SERVES 12–14)

PREP: 45 MINUTES
CHILL: 1 HOUR
BAKE: 25 MINUTES

For the sponge

225g self-raising flour

1 tsp baking powder

½ tsp sea salt

175g unsalted butter, softened, plus extra for greasing

175g golden caster sugar

1 tsp vanilla extract or bean paste

4 medium eggs

75g full-fat Greek yoghurt

2 tbsp milk

For the buttercream

350g unsalted butter, softened

2 tsp vanilla bean paste

700g icing sugar, sifted

Food colouring of your choice (a mix of blue and green looks lovely to give a duck-egg-blue effect, but any pastel colours will work)

2–3 tbsp milk

1 Grease and line three 15cm (6in) round tins, or use silicone moulds.

2 To make the sponge, mix the flour, baking powder and salt together in a large bowl.

3 In a separate bowl, beat the butter, sugar and vanilla together until pale and fluffy. Add the eggs one at a time, beating well after each addition. Don't worry if the mixture curdles a little. Beat in the yoghurt, then fold through the flour until smooth and loosen with the milk. Divide the mixture equally between the prepared tins.

4 Preheat the air fryer to 140°C. Bake for 20–25 minutes, or until well risen and golden. A skewer inserted into the centre should come out clean. Leave to cool in the tins for 5 minutes, then turn out onto wire racks to cool completely.

5 To make the buttercream, beat the butter and vanilla in the bowl of a stand mixer fitted with a paddle beater (or use an electric hand whisk and beat on high for about 1 minute, or beat by hand with a wooden spoon and a lot of elbow grease) until very creamy and smooth. Add the icing sugar, about one-quarter at a time, beating between each addition on slow at first so that the icing sugar doesn't puff up everywhere, then increase the speed to high for about 1 minute. Mix in the food colouring to achieve a lovely pastel shade. Loosen with the milk to get a soft, spreadable consistency. Cover with clingfilm or a damp tea towel to prevent the surface crusting over and set aside.

6 If the cakes have humps from the rise, level them off with a bread knife or cake leveller. Place the first cake onto a stand, board or plate and spread over a layer of buttercream. Position the second cake on top, lining it up neatly, and spread over another layer of buttercream. Place the last cake on top, smooth-side up. Press down gently with the palm of your hand to secure the sponges together.

recipe continued overleaf . . .

For the speckling detail

½ tsp cocoa powder

1 tsp vanilla extract

TIP

*Use this
recipe to make
a 20cm (8in)
2-layer cake if
you prefer.*

7   Using a palette knife, generously spread more buttercream around the sides of the cakes, then spread an even layer over the top of the cake. Once the whole cake is covered, clean the palette knife and go around the cake again to smooth off any excess until you are happy the finish is neat. Put the cake in the fridge for about 30 minutes to chill and firm up.

8   For the final layer of icing, repeat the crumb coating process above, but use a slightly thicker layer of buttercream. Paddle around the sides and over the top until you are happy with the covering. Refrigerate for a further 30 minutes.

9   For the speckling detail, mix the cocoa powder and vanilla together to make a thick liquid. Dip a clean paintbrush or pastry brush into the liquid, then bend back the bristles and 'flick' the chocolatey liquid up against the sides and over the top of the cake until you have a lovely, speckled pattern. Decorate with mini chocolate eggs.

10 The cake will keep for 3 days, or can be frozen for up to a month.

Adaptations

(DF) *Substitute the butter for vegan block butter or spread, use non-dairy yoghurt and plant milk.*

(GF) *Substitute the flour for a gluten-free blend.*

EASTER NEST CUPCAKES

I love Easter baking season! It's like Christmas but without the hassle of having to think of gift ideas! These cupcakes are brilliant because you fill the little buttercream swirls with a mix of mini chocolate eggs. They are fun to make and look effective, and the kids will love helping out! Expect chocolate fingerprints everywhere though.

MAKES 12–16 CUPCAKES

PREP: 25 MINUTES
BAKE: 15 MINUTES

For the sponge

200g margarine or spreadable butter

200g golden caster sugar

4 medium eggs

175g self-raising flour

30g cocoa powder, sifted

1 tsp baking powder

¼ tsp sea salt

75g buttermilk or full-fat yoghurt

For the buttercream

300g unsalted butter, softened

650g icing sugar, sifted

2 tsp vanilla extract or bean paste

60g cocoa powder

2–3 tbsp just-boiled water

To decorate

Mini chocolate eggs of your choice

1   Line two or three six-hole cupcake tins with paper cases, or use individual silicone moulds.

2   Start by making the sponge. Beat the margarine and sugar together until really pale, fluffy and creamy. Add the eggs one at a time, beating well after each addition.

3   In a separate bowl, combine the flour, cocoa powder, baking powder and salt, then add this to the wet mixture. Add the buttermilk and beat on slow until the batter is smooth. Divide the batter equally between the cupcake cases.

4   Preheat the air fryer to 150°C. Bake for 10–15 minutes until cooked through. Turn upside-down if the bottoms feel a little soggy for the final 2 minutes. Leave to cool in the cases for 5 minutes, then turn out onto a wire rack to cool completely.

5   To make the buttercream, beat the butter, icing sugar and vanilla together until pale and fluffy. In a small bowl, mix the cocoa powder and hot water to a thick paste, then add to the buttercream. Add a little extra water if you need to make the paste a little looser – it should be soft and pipeable, but not runny.

6   Load the buttercream into a piping bag fitted with a large star nozzle (I use Wilton 4b). Holding the bag vertically, start piping in the centre and wind outwards towards the edge of the cupcakes. Build up around the edge with another circle of buttercream to create a chocolatey nest. Fill with mini eggs and serve. These will keep in an airtight container for up to 3 days.

Adaptations

(DF) *Substitute the butter for vegan block butter or spread and use non-dairy yoghurt and dairy-free chocolate eggs.*

(GF) *Substitute the flour for a gluten-free blend.*

MONSTER COOKIES

Stand by for some ghostly goings-on in the kitchen! These are so much fun for Halloween or spooky gatherings, and a great way to get the whole family involved. You can make one colour dough for ease, or split the dough and make a mix – get the kids involved making their own colours. For a larger gathering, double or triple the quantities as needed. The dough balls keep in the fridge for up to 3 days, or can be frozen.

MAKES 10–12 COOKIES

PREP: 20 MINUTES
BAKE: 12 MINUTES

125g salted butter, at room temperature

75g light muscovado sugar

75g caster sugar

1 tsp vanilla bean paste

1 medium egg

180g plain flour

1 tsp baking powder

150g white chocolate chips or chopped chocolate

Food colouring gels (green, orange and purple)

To decorate

Smarties or colourful chocolates for the eyes (or shop-bought sugar eyes)

Black edible marker pen or black icing

1 Line the air fryer baking trays with parchment paper or silicone liners.

2 Using a stand mixer or electric hand mixer on medium speed, cream the butter, both sugars and vanilla until pale and fluffy, or cream by hand with a wooden spoon. Reduce the speed to slow and beat in the egg until combined. Tip in the flour and baking powder and mix until combined and you have a sticky dough. Drop in the chocolate and briefly mix on slow to distribute.

3 Split the dough into bowls and tint with a few drops of food colouring gel. I used green, orange and purple, or just stick to one colour if you prefer.

4 Roll a large walnut-sized piece of dough into a ball. The dough is quite sticky, so dampen your hands first. Pop onto a plate and refrigerate to firm up a little (once firm, you can freeze them if you wish).

5 Place the cookies on the trays. They will double in diameter when baked, so allow plenty of space between. Bake for 10–12 minutes, pressing down gently to flatten with a spatula about halfway through the bake. The cookies should be lightly golden around the edges but still a bit squidgy in the centre.

6 While still slightly warm and squidgy, press the Smarties or eyes into the cookies to create googly eyes. Draw little dots for the pupils using a black edible marker pen or black icing.

7 Allow to cool on the trays for a few minutes before serving. These will keep for up to 5 days in an airtight container.

Adaptation

(DF) *Substitute the butter for vegan block butter.*

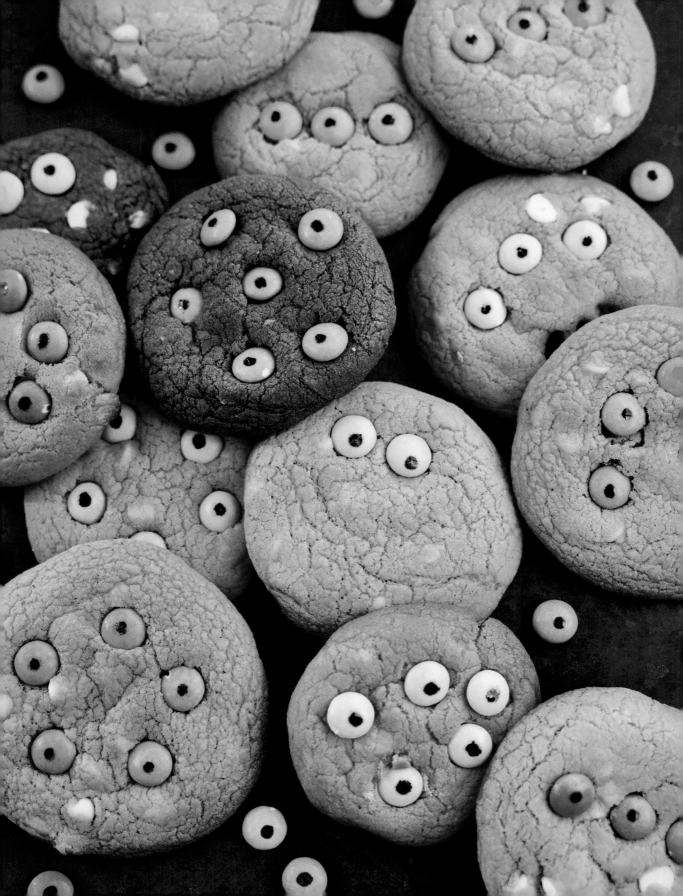

PUMPKIN SPICED HALLOWEEN TRAYBAKE

Boo! This is ideal for a Halloween party. You can buy decorations, but if you want to make yours look really special, you can make your own.

SERVES 16–20
PREP: 45 MINUTES
BAKE: 35 MINUTES

For the pumpkin spice mix

3 tbsp ground cinnamon

2 tsp ground ginger

2 tsp ground nutmeg

1½ tsp ground allspice

½ tsp ground cloves

For the sponge

225g vegetable oil

125g light brown sugar

125g caster sugar

5 medium eggs

1½ tsp vanilla extract

425g can pumpkin purée

350g self-raising flour

1 tsp sea salt

For the icing

750g icing sugar, sifted

325g butter, softened

2–3 tbsp milk

2–4 food colourings of your choice

For the decorations

Icing sugar, for dusting

75g white, orange and black sugarpaste

Halloween sprinkles

1 To make the sugarpaste decorations, dust a work surface with icing sugar, roll out the icing and cut/shape into eyes, pumpkins and bats using cutters or a knife. For googly eyes, make white balls, flatten and add black dots for pupils. Set aside to dry.

2 Line a 9x13cm (3½x5in) baking tray with parchment paper.

3 To make the pumpkin spice mix, combine all the spices in a small jar.

4 To make the sponge, mix the oil, both sugars, eggs, vanilla and pumpkin purée together in a large bowl.

5 In a separate bowl, mix the flour, salt and 1 tablespoon of the pumpkin spice mix. Tip the dry ingredients into the wet and whisk until combined. Pour the batter into the prepared baking tray.

6 Preheat the air fryer to 150°C. Bake for 30–35 minutes until a skewer inserted into the centre comes out clean.

7 Meanwhile, make the icing. Put one-fifth of the icing sugar in the bowl of a stand mixer, then add the butter. Mix on a low speed until the butter is incorporated, then increase the speed to high and beat until light and fluffy, or beat by hand with a wooden spoon. Add half the remaining icing sugar and 1 tablespoon of the pumpkin spice mix and beat on slow until incorporated, then increase to a high speed and beat again. Add the remaining icing sugar and repeat the process. Loosen with a little milk to achieve a soft, pipeable consistency.

8 Separate the icing into smaller bowls and stir your chosen food colourings into each. Put the coloured icing into piping bags with different-shape piping nozzles – large open stars (Wilton 1m), petal nozzle (Wilton 126) and Large 1cm Round nozzle – and pipe all over the cake using different piping techniques. Finish with Halloween sprinkles and the sugar decorations if you wish.

CARROT PATCH CAKE

A deliciously moist carrot cake made to look like a carrot patch using fresh mini carrots with their tops on and some cocoa-dusted chopped nuts for the earth – simple yet effective. If Beatrix Potter had a favourite cake, then this would be it.

MAKES 20CM (8IN) 2-LAYER ROUND CAKE (SERVES 12–14)
PREP: 30 MINUTES
BAKE: 30 MINUTES

For the sponge

185g light muscovado sugar

185g sunflower oil, plus extra for greasing

3 medium eggs

125g carrot, grated

120g sultanas

50g glacé ginger or stem ginger, chopped

Zest of 1 orange

220g self-raising flour

1 tsp bicarbonate of soda

¼ tsp sea salt

2 tsp ground cinnamon

1 tsp ground ginger

For the icing

100g unsalted butter, softened

100g cream cheese, at room temperature

1 tsp vanilla bean paste

200g icing sugar, sieved

1 tbsp chopped walnuts or pecans

1 tsp cocoa powder

Raw baby carrots with tops

1 Grease and line two 20cm (8in) round cake tins, or use silicone moulds.

2 Start by making the sponge. In a large bowl, whisk the sugar into the oil until any large lumps have disappeared. Add the eggs and whisk through until smooth. Tip in the grated carrot, sultanas, glacé ginger and orange zest and mix together with a spoon.

3 Put the flour in a separate bowl and fork through the bicarbonate of soda, salt and spices, then add this to the wet mixture and gently combine until just mixed. Divide equally between the tins.

4 Preheat the air fryer to 150°C. Bake for 25–30 minutes until golden, springy and cooked through. Leave to cool in the tins for 5 minutes, then turn out onto a wire rack to cool completely.

5 To make the icing, beat the butter, cream cheese and vanilla together until pale, smooth and creamy, then gently beat in the icing sugar in two batches.

6 If the cakes have a little hump from the rise, trim the tops to level them. Place one cake trimmed-side up on a plate, board or stand, and spread or pipe over with a layer of icing. Place the second cake on top and cover generously with icing.

7 In a bowl, toss the chopped nuts in the cocoa powder, then crumble over the cake where you want the 'soil' to be. Wash, dry and trim the carrots down to different lengths, cut down the green tops a little and place around the top of the cake in a pretty pattern, as if they are growing out from the cake.

PIÑATA PARTY CUPCAKES

Perfect for any party, or a fun activity to do with the kids. I love this sponge recipe – it's rich and soft, unlike some recipes that can be very dry. The secret to a great chocolate cake is to slightly underbake it. Look for a very slight 'wobble factor' in the middle.

MAKES 10–12 CUPCAKES

PREP: 30 MINUTES
BAKE: 15 MINUTES

For the sponge

120g plain chocolate chips

135g light muscovado sugar

120g salted butter, softened

2 medium eggs, plus 1 egg yolk

70g soured cream or full-fat plain yoghurt

1 tsp vanilla extract or bean paste

100g self-raising flour

20g cocoa powder

Mini sweets and/or chocolates and sprinkles (about 1 tsp per cake)

For the buttercream

200g soft unsalted butter

1 tsp vanilla bean paste or extract

400g sifted icing sugar

To decorate

Sprinkles

1   Line two six-hole cupcake tins with paper cases, or use individual silicone moulds.

2   Put the chocolate chips, sugar and butter in a heatproof bowl. Microwave on a medium heat in 30-second bursts, stirring between each, until all melted. Alternatively, melt in a heatproof bowl set over a pan of simmering water. Do not allow the base of the bowl to touch the water. Set aside to cool slightly.

3   In a small bowl, whisk the eggs and yolk, soured cream and vanilla together. In a separate bowl, mix the flour and cocoa powder to combine.

4   Add the egg mixture to the melted chocolate and stir well. Fold in the flour and cocoa. Spoon into 10–12 cupcake cases to just over half to two-thirds full.

5   Preheat the air fryer to 150°C. Bake for 12–15 minutes until just firm. A skewer inserted into the centre should come out slightly sticky but not wet, as you want a fudgy sponge. Leave to cool in the tins.

6   Meanwhile make the buttercream by beating the butter and vanilla until pale and creamy, then gradually add the icing sugar, beating between each addition. Beat until fluffy, pale and smooth, set aside covered with cling film or a damp tea towel or load into your piping bag ready for piping onto the cakes.

7   Once cooled, carefully spoon out a core from the centre of the cakes (or use an apple corer) to create a hole in the middle of each cake, saving the pieces you've removed. Fill with your favourite sweets or chocolate almost to the top, then cut the top off the cores and plug the holes to conceal the surprise centre. Top with swirls of buttercream and plenty of sprinkles!

Adaptation

GF *Substitute the flour for a gluten-free blend.*

FUNFETTI BUTTERCREAM BIRTHDAY CAKE

I'm obsessed with Funfetti cakes, and to me, a sprinkling on the inside and outside of a cake is the epitome of a classic birthday cake. An explosion of colour, a bit like a rainbow mated with a Victoria sponge!

MAKES 20CM (8IN) 3-LAYER ROUND CAKE (SERVES 16)

PREP: 45 MINUTES
BAKE: 25 MINUTES

For the sponge

300g margarine or spreadable butter, plus extra for greasing

300g caster sugar

2 tsp vanilla extract or bean paste

6 medium eggs

300g self-raising flour

½ tsp sea salt

1 tsp baking powder

75g milk

3–4 tbsp Funfetti or bright cake sprinkles (ensure they are 'bake stable', so they hold their colour and shape when baked – I used Truly Sprinkles)

For the buttercream

500g unsalted butter, softened

2 tsp vanilla extract or bean paste

1kg icing sugar

To decorate

Extra sprinkles

1 Grease and line three 20cm (8in) round cake tins, or use silicone moulds.

2 Start by making the sponge. Beat the margarine, sugar and vanilla on a high speed for a few minutes until very pale, really creamy and fluffy. Add the eggs one at a time, beating well after each addition.

3 In a separate bowl, whisk the flour, salt and baking powder together. Add to the margarine mixture in three batches, only just incorporating each time, then loosen with the milk. Stir in the sprinkles. Divide the mixture equally between the tins and level off with a spatula.

4 Preheat the air fryer to 160°C. Bake for 20–25 minutes, or until cooked through, risen and spongy. Leave to cool in the tin for 5 minutes, then turn out onto a wire rack to cool completely.

5 To make the buttercream, beat the butter, vanilla and icing sugar until really pale, creamy and fluffy.

6 Trim the top of the cakes to flatten, if needed. Fill and crumb coat as described on p23, then add a second coat.

7 To decorate the cake, hold the sprinkles in your hand and with a flat palm, press them up against the side of the cake, creating a wavy band around the edge, or if you have lots of sprinkles, you can coat the whole side and top. Use a knife to push in any strays, and brush off any excess. To make it extra fancy, you can add buttercream to a piping bag fitted with a star nozzle and pipe a rope border or rosettes around the top outside edge of the cake and sprinkle with more Funfetti.

Adaptations

(DF) *Substitute the butter for vegan block butter and use plant milk.*

(GF) *Substitute the flour for a gluten-free blend.*

PULL-APART CUPCAKE FLOWERS

Pull-apart cakes are a brilliant way to make a large party cake without the need to bake in large tins. You can create so many designs like this. I've opted for a collection of flowers in pretty colours. The great thing about this is that you don't have to slice up a cake – guests can just help themselves!

MAKES 24 CUPCAKES TO MAKE 3 FLOWERS
PREP: 45 MINUTES
BAKE: 18 MINUTES

For the sponge

250g self-raising flour

60g desiccated coconut

1 tsp baking powder

¼ tsp sea salt

150g coconut oil

320g golden caster sugar

5 medium eggs

125g full-fat coconut milk from a can

Zest and juice of 2 limes

For the buttercream

450g unsalted butter, softened

130g coconut cream

Zest of 2 limes and juice of 1

900g icing sugar, sifted

Food colouring of choice

1   Line four six-hole cupcake tins with paper cases, or use individual silicone moulds. (You will have to make this cake in batches.)

2   Mix the flour, desiccated coconut, baking powder and salt together.

3   Put the coconut oil and sugar in a separate large bowl and beat using an electric whisk for about 5 minutes until light and creamy. Add the eggs one at a time, beating well after each addition. Shake the coconut milk or stir well. Stir in half the flour mixture, then half the coconut milk, then repeat with the rest of the flour mixture and coconut milk. Gently mix in the lime zest and juice.

4   Divide the batter into the cupcake cases, filling to just under two-thirds full. Preheat the air fryer to 160°C. Bake for 14–18 minutes, or until the cakes are golden. If you need to, turn them over for the last couple of minutes to ensure the undersides are fully cooked. Remove from the tin and transfer to a wire rack to cool completely.

5   To make the buttercream, beat the butter, coconut cream and lime zest together until pale and creamy. Add the icing sugar in two batches, beating until pale and fluffy. Beat in the lime juice.

6   Each flower is made up of eight cupcakes – one for the centre, six for the petals and one off to the side as a leaf. You can make the petals all one colour or a mix of shades. Tint 150g of the icing yellow for the centres; 150g green for the leaves; then divide the remaining icing into 3 equal portions and tint each to your preferred colours for the petals.

7   Pipe the petals by holding the piping bag (1m nozzle) vertically to the cakes, begin in the middle and swirl out to the edge. Fill in the middles with little dots (5mm snip in the bag). Lastly, pipe 3 leaves on the last three cupcakes with a large V nozzle (1cm round) or V cut in the bag, squeezing across the cake and leaving a point for each leaf. These will keep for a few days in an airtight container, or can be frozen for up to a month.

Adaptation

(DF) *Substitute the butter for vegan block butter.*

COFFEE CREAM HEART CAKE

No special heart tin needed here, just use this clever hack! This cake is the perfect way to tell someone you love them, or make it just because you love heart shapes. It's great to customise for any time of year – dress it with fresh berries, edible flowers and petals, sprinkles or sweets. I've used dried edible flower petals on my cake.

MAKES 20CM (8IN) 2-LAYER ROUND CAKE (SERVES 12–14)

PREP: 1 HOUR
CHILL: 1 HOUR
BAKE: 25 MINUTES

For the sponge (all at room temperature)

200g margarine or spreadable butter, plus extra for greasing

200g caster sugar

2 tsp vanilla bean paste

2 tbsp strong espresso coffee, cooled

4 medium eggs

225g self-raising flour and 1 tsp baking powder

125g buttermilk

For the icing (all at room temperature)

350g unsalted butter, softened

200g cream cheese

750g icing sugar, sifted

2 tsp vanilla bean paste

2 tbsp strong espresso coffee, cooled

To decorate

Edible flowers or sugar-coated chocolates

1 Grease and line two 20cm (8in) round tins, or use silicone moulds.

2 To make the sponge, cream the butter, sugar and vanilla until pale and fluffy. Beat in the coffee. Add the eggs one at a time, beating after each addition. Fold in half the flour, then half the buttermilk. Repeat with the remaining flour and buttermilk. Divide the batter equally between the tins and level off.

3 Preheat the air fryer to 150°C. Bake for 20–25 minutes until the tops spring back when lightly touched and the sponge is cooked through. Leave to cool in the tins for 5 minutes, then turn out onto a wire rack to cool completely.

4 To make the icing, beat the butter and cream cheese together, then gradually add the icing sugar, beating well after each addition, until pale and fluffy. Add the vanilla and coffee and whisk until smooth and creamy.

5 To assemble, sandwich the cakes with some icing and smooth around the sides. Refrigerate for about 30 minutes to set.

6 Cut into a heart shape by lightly marking out quarters on the top of the cake using a bread knife, to form a cross. Remove two 'humps' from one side of the cake by cutting from 12 to 3 o'clock and removing the rounded part, then repeat from 12 to 9 o'clock.

7 Add more icing to the rounded part you didn't cut, and stick the offcuts to the rounded edge with more icing. Smooth all around the shape with icing to cover any gaps and seal in the crumbs. Cut a little V shape into the heart at the top to accentuate the shape, then smooth over with more icing. Chill for a further 30 minutes.

8 Spread the remaining icing over the top and sides, using a palette knife to make swirls and flicks in the icing. Decorate with edible flower petals, fresh or dried. The cake will keep in the fridge for up to 3 days. Bring to room temperature before serving.

Adaptation

GF *Substitute the flour for a gluten-free blend.*

TIP
Halve the ingredients if you want to make a smaller 15cm (6in) 2-layer round cake. Bake for 15–18 minutes.

INDEX

A

almonds: Apricot Tart 106
    Banana and Chocolate Muffins 83
    Banana, Pecan and Caramel Bread 73
    Cherry and Almond Cake 62
apples: Quick Apple Tart 103
apricots: Apricot Custard Danish Pastries 101
    Apricot Tart 106

B

babka bread: Garlic and Herb Cheesy Babka Bread 146
bacon: Mum's Quiche 111–12
bananas: Banana and Chocolate Muffins 83
    Banana, Pecan and Caramel Bread 73
baps: Breakfast Baps 151
beetroot: Chocolate and Beetroot Cake 86
berries: Pavlova 137–8
    Pistachio and Ricotta Cake 87
birthday cake: Funfetti Buttercream Birthday Cake 212
Biscoff: Biscoff Brownies 75
    Cinnamon Spiced Tahini Xmas Cake 191–2
biscuits & cookies 26–57
    Bourbon Biscuits 32
    Chewy Chocolate Chip Cookies 36
    Christmas Pudding Cookies 180
    Cookies 'n' Cream Cheesecakes 126
    Custard Creams 34
    Funfetti Cookies 50
    Giant Cookie Pie 140
    Jammie Dodgers 31
    Millionaire's Shortbread 28
    Mocha Choc Coffee Whoopie Pies 38
    Monster Cookies 204
    Oaty Raisin Cookies 40
    Parmesan and Thyme Biscuits 56
    Party Rings 53–4
    Salted Caramel-Stuffed Cookies 49
    Slice-and-Bake Chocolate and Hazelnut Freezer Cookies 43
    Strawberries and Cream Shortbread Stacks 44
    Thumb Print Cookies 55
    Viennese Whirls 46
Blackberry Crumbles 139
Blueberry Lemon Cake 76
Bourbon Biscuits 32
brandy: Christmas Cake 178
bread: Breadgehog Rolls 166
    Breakfast Baps 151
    Easy 50/50 Loaf 153
    Easy Flatbreads 161
    Fluffy Dinner Rolls 148–50
    Focaccia 158–60
    Garlic and Herb Cheesy Babka Bread 146
    Overnight No-Knead Fridge Bread 157
    scaling recipes 17
    Soda Bread 154
bread and butter pudding: Croissant Bread and Butter Pudding 142
Breadgehog Rolls 166
breadsticks: Olive and Tomato Breadsticks 155
Breakfast Baps 151
Broccoli Cheese Puffs 123
brownies: Biscoff brownies 75
Bruce Chocolate Fudge Cake 70–2
bundt cake: Clotted Cream Bundt Cake 91
buns: Cinnamon Buns 169–70
    Hot Cross Buns 197–9
    Iced Buns 174–5
butter: Cheese-Stuffed Garlic Dough Balls 163–4
buttercream, scaling recipes 16–17
buttermilk: Coffee Cream Heart Cake 216
    Easter Nest Cupcakes 203
    Gingerbread Latte Cupcakes 188–9
    Red Velvet Cupcakes 80–2
    Soda Bread 154

C

cakes: Banana, Pecan and Caramel Bread 73
    Biscoff Brownies 75
    Blueberry Lemon Cake 76
    Bruce Chocolate Fudge Cake 70–2
    Candy Cane Forest Showstopper Christmas Cake 184–6
    Carrot Patch Cake 208
    Cherry and Almond Cake 62
    Chocolate and Beetroot Cake 86
    Chocolate Peanut Butter Cake 65–6
    Christmas Cake 178
    Cinnamon Spiced Tahini Xmas Cake 191–2
    Classic Victoria Sponge 84
    Clotted Cream Bundt Cake 91
    Coffee and Walnut Squares 79
    Coffee Cream Heart Cake 216
    Funfetti Buttercream Birthday Cake 212
    icing and decorating 20–5
    Lemon Drizzle Cake 67
    Olive Oil Cake 92
    Pineapple Upside-Down Cake 88
    Pistachio and Ricotta Cake 87
    Pumpkin Spiced Halloween Traybake 207
    scaling recipes 15–17
    Speckled Egg Cake 200–2
    see also cupcakes; muffins
Candied Orange Slices 196
Candy Cane Forest Showstopper Christmas Cake 184–6
capers: Tapenade Palmiers 119
caramel: Banana, Pecan and Caramel Bread 73
    Millionaire's Shortbread 28
    Salted Caramel-Stuffed Cookies 49
carrots: Carrot Patch Cake 208
    Vegetable Rose Tarts 115
Chantilly cream: Choux Buns 109

Cheat's Danish Pastries
– 3 Ways 101–2
cheese: Broccoli Cheese Puffs 123
   Cheese and Marmite
   Muffins 94
   Cheese and Spring
   Onion Scones 93
   Cheese-Stuffed Garlic
   Dough Balls 163–4
   Garlic and Herb Cheesy
   Babka Bread 146
   Leek, Cheese and
   Potato Pie 114
   Leftover Cheeseboard
   Straws 193
   Mum's Quiche 111–12
   Parmesan and Thyme
   Biscuits 56
   Pizza Pinwheels 165
   Roasted Tomato and
   Mozzarella Puff Pastry Tart 118
   Spinach and Feta Swirls 122
   Tapenade Palmiers 119
   Tomato Galette 116
   Vegetable Rose Tarts 115
   see also cream cheese;
   mascarpone; ricotta cheese
cheesecakes: Mini Cookies
'n' Cream Cheesecakes 126
   New York Baked
   Cheesecake 129
cherries: Cherry and
Almond Cake 62
   Christmas Cake 178
   Pina Colada Cupcakes 68
   Pineapple Upside-
   Down Cake 88
cherry pie filling: Cherry
Hand Pies 107
Chewy Chocolate
Chip Cookies 36
chocolate: Banana and
Chocolate Muffins 83
   Biscoff Brownies 75
   Bourbon Biscuits 32
   Bruce Chocolate
   Fudge Cake 70–2
   Candy Cane Forest
   Showstopper Christmas
   Cake 184–6
   Chewy Chocolate
   Chip Cookies 36

Chocolate and
Beetroot Cake 86
Chocolate Fondants 143
Chocolate Ganache
Tartlets 98
Chocolate Orange
Cupcakes 195–6
Chocolate Peanut
Butter Cake 65–6
Choux Buns 109
Christmas Pudding
Cookies 180
Classic Chocolate-Glazed
Doughnuts 171–2
Croissant Bread and
Butter Pudding 142
Easter Nest Cupcakes 203
Giant Cookie Pie 140
Millionaire's Shortbread 28
Mocha Choc Coffee
Whoopie Pies 38
Monster Cookies 204
Pavlova 137–8
Piñata Party Cupcakes 211
Red Velvet Cupcakes 80–2
Salted Caramel-
Stuffed Cookies 49
Slice-and-Bake Chocolate and
Hazelnut Freezer Cookies 43
Viennese Whirls 46
Choux Buns 109
Christmas Cake 178
   Candy Cane Forest
   Showstopper Christmas
   Cake 184–6
   Cinnamon Spiced Tahini
   Xmas Cake 191–2
Christmas Pudding Cookies 180
cinnamon: Cinnamon
Buns 169–70
   Cinnamon Spiced Tahini
   Xmas Cake 191–2
   Pumpkin Spiced Halloween
   Traybake 207
Classic Chocolate-Glazed
Doughnuts 171–2
Classic Scones 60
Classic Victoria Sponge 84
Clotted Cream Bundt Cake 91
cobbler: Peach and
Raspberry Cobbler 130

coconut: Pull-Apart
Cupcake Flowers 215
coconut cream: Pina
Colada Cupcakes 68
   Pull-Apart Cupcake
   Flowers 215
coffee: Coffee and
Walnut Squares 79
   Coffee Cream Heart Cake 216
   Mocha Choc Coffee
   Whoopie Pies 38
coffee syrup: Gingerbread
Latte Cupcakes 188–9
condensed milk: Millionaire's
Shortbread 28
cookies see biscuits & cookies
cornflakes: Flapjacks 41
courgettes: Vegetable
Rose Tarts 115
Courvoisier: Mince Pies 187
cream: Bruce Chocolate
Fudge Cake 70–2
   Chocolate and
   Beetroot Cake 86
   Chocolate Ganache
   Tartlets 98
   Chocolate Peanut
   Butter Cake 65–6
   Choux Buns 109
   Classic Scones 60
   Classic Victoria Sponge 84
   Clotted Cream Bundt Cake 91
   Croissant Bread and
   Butter Pudding 142
   Easy Strawberry Tart 104
   Mum's Quiche 111–12
   Pavlova 137–8
   Self-Saucing Sticky
   Toffee Pudding 135
   Strawberries and Cream
   Shortbread Stacks 44
cream cheese: Carrot
Patch Cake 208
   Cinnamon Buns 169–70
   Coffee and Walnut Squares 79
   Coffee Cream Heart Cake 216
   Gingerbread Latte
   Cupcakes 188–9
   Mini Cookies 'n' Cream
   Cheesecakes 126
   Mocha Choc Coffee

Whoopie Pies 38
New York Baked
Cheesecake 129
Red Velvet Cupcakes 80–2
Croissant Bread and
Butter Pudding 142
crumb coat method 23
crumble: Blackberry
Crumbles 139
cupcakes: Chocolate
Orange Cupcakes 195–6
Easter Nest Cupcakes 203
Elf Spaghetti Cupcakes 183
Gingerbread Latte
Cupcakes 188–9
icing 25
Pina Colada Cupcakes 68
Piñata Party Cupcakes 211
Pull-Apart Cupcake
Flowers 215
Red Velvet Cupcakes 80–2
scaling recipes 16
see also muffins
curds: Thumb Print Cookies 55
currants: Christmas Cake 178
custard: Apricot Custard
Danish Pastries 101
Custard Creams 34

D
Danish pastries: Apricot
Custard Danish Pastries 101
Cheat's Danish pastries 101–2
Pecan and Maple Twists 101–2
Raisin Swirls 101–2
dates: Self-Saucing Sticky
Toffee Pudding 135
decorating bakes 20–5
digestive biscuits: New York
Baked Cheesecake 129
dough: Cheese-Stuffed
Garlic Dough Balls 163–4
scaling recipes 17
doughnuts: Classic Chocolate-
Glazed Doughnuts 171–2

E
Easter: Easter Nest
Cupcakes 203
Hot Cross Buns 197–9
Speckled Egg Cake 200–2

Easy 50/50 Loaf 153
Easy Flatbreads 161
Easy Strawberry Tart 104
eggs: Pavlova 137–8
scaling recipes 15
Elf Spaghetti Cupcakes 183
equipment 11–14

F
fennel seeds: Leek, Cheese
and Potato Pie 114
feta cheese: Spinach
and Feta Swirls 122
filo pastry: Spinach
and Feta Swirls 122
Flapjacks 41
flatbreads: Easy Flatbreads
161
Focaccia 158–60
Fluffy Dinner Rolls 148–50
Focaccia 158–60
fondants: Chocolate
fondants 143
freezer cookies: Slice-and-
Bake Chocolate and Hazelnut
Freezer Cookies 43
fridge bread: Overnight No-
Knead Fridge Bread 157
fruit: Pavlova 137–8
Pistachio and Ricotta Cake 87
fudge: Bruce Chocolate
Fudge Cake 70–2
Funfetti: Funfetti Buttercream
Birthday Cake 212
Funfetti Cookies 50

G
galette: Tomato Galette 116
ganache: Chocolate
Ganache filling 98
scaling recipes 16–17
garlic: Cheese-Stuffed
Garlic Dough Balls 163–4
Focaccia 158–60
Garlic and Herb Cheesy
Babka Bread 146
Giant Cookie Pie 140
ginger: Carrot Patch Cake 208
Christmas Cake 178
Christmas Pudding
Cookies 180

Gingerbread Latte
Cupcakes 188–9
Hot Cross Buns 197–9
Gingerbread Latte
Cupcakes 188–9
glacé cherries: Christmas
Cake 178
Pineapple Upside-
Down Cake 88
golden syrup: Syrup
Sponge Puddings 132

H
Halloween: Monster Cookies 204
Pumpkin Spiced Halloween
Traybake 207
hand pies: Cherry Hand Pies 107
hazelnut crème spread: Croissant
Bread and Butter Pudding 142
hazelnuts: Slice-and-Bake
Chocolate and Hazelnut
Freezer Cookies 43
herbs: Garlic and Herb
Cheesy Babka Bread 146
Hot Cross Buns 197–9

I
Iced Buns 174–5
icing: icing bakes 20–5
icing styles 25
scaling recipes 16–17

J
jam: Apricot Custard
Danish Pastries 101
Apricot Tart 106
Blueberry Lemon Cake 76
Classic Scones 60
Classic Victoria Sponge 84
Easy Strawberry Tart 104
Jam Sponge Pudding 134
Jam Tarts 110
Jammie Dodgers 31
Quick Apple Tart 103
Raisin Swirls 101–2
Thumb Print Cookies 55
Viennese Whirls 46
Jammie Dodgers 31

L

lavender: Clotted Cream
Bundt Cake 91
layer cakes, rough-icing 20–1
Leek, Cheese and Potato Pie 114
Leftover Cheeseboard Straws 193
lemons: Blueberry
Lemon Cake 76
    Lemon Drizzle Cake 67
limes: Pull-Apart Cupcake
Flowers 215

M

Malibu: Pina Colada
Cupcakes 68
maple syrup: Elf Spaghetti
Cupcakes 183
    Pecan and Maple Twists 101–2
Marmite: Cheese and
Marmite Muffins 94
marzipan: Gingerbread
Latte Cupcakes 188–9
mascarpone cheese: Easy
Strawberry Tart 104
    Vegetable Rose Tarts 115
meringues: Pavlova 137–8
Millionaire's Shortbread 28
Mince Pies 187
Mini Cookies 'n' Cream
Cheesecakes 126
mixed peel: Christmas Cake 178
    Hot Cross Buns 197–9
Mocha Choc Coffee
Whoopie Pies 38
Monster Cookies 204
mozzarella: Cheese-Stuffed
Garlic Dough Balls 163–4
    Garlic and Herb Cheesy
    Babka Bread 146
    Pizza Pinwheels 165
    Roasted Tomato and
    Mozzarella Puff Pastry Tart 118
muffins: Banana and
Chocolate Muffins 83
    Cheese and Marmite
    Muffins 94
    see also cupcakes
Mum's Quiche 111–12

N

naked cakes 23
New York Baked Cheesecake 129
nuts: Chocolate Peanut
Butter Cake 65–6

O

oat milk: Biscoff Brownies 75
oats: Banana and
Chocolate Muffins 83
    Blackberry Crumbles 139
    Flapjacks 41
    Oaty Raisin Cookies 40
Olive Oil Cake 92
olives: Breadgehog Rolls 166
    Focaccia 158–60
    Olive and Tomato
    Breadsticks 155
    Tapenade Palmiers 119
oranges: Candied
Orange Slices 196
    Carrot Patch Cake 208
    Chocolate Orange
    Cupcakes 195–6
    Mince Pies 187
    Olive Oil Cake 92
    Pistachio and Ricotta Cake 87
Oreo cookies: Mini Cookies
'n' Cream Cheesecakes 126
Overnight No-Knead
Fridge Bread 157

P

palmiers: Tapenade Palmiers 119
Parmesan: Parmesan and
Thyme Biscuits 56
Vegetable Rose Tarts 115
Party Rings 53–4
pastries: Apricot Custard
Danish Pastries 101
    Broccoli Cheese Puffs 123
    Cheat's Danish Pastries
    – 3 Ways 101–2
    Leftover Cheeseboard
    Straws 193
    Pecan and Maple Twists 101–2
    Raisin Swirls 101–2
    Sausage Rolls 121
    Spinach and Feta Swirls 122
    Tapenade Palmiers 119

pastry, choux 109
Pavlova 137–8
Peach and Raspberry
Cobbler 130
peanut butter: Chocolate
Peanut Butter Cake 65–6
peanuts: Chocolate
Ganache Tartlets 98
pecans: Banana, Pecan
and Caramel Bread 73
    Pecan and Maple Twists 101–2
peppermint extract: Candy
Cane Forest Showstopper
Christmas Cake 184–6
pesto: Roasted Tomato and
Mozzarella Puff Pastry Tart 118
    Vegetable Rose Tarts 115
pies: Cherry Hand Pies 107
    Giant Cookie Pie 140
    Leek, Cheese and
    Potato Pie 114
    Mince Pies 187
Pina Colada Cupcakes 68
Piñata Party Cupcakes 211
pineapple: Pina Colada
Cupcakes 68
    Pineapple Upside-
    Down Cake 88
pinwheels: Pizza Pinwheels 165
Pistachio and Ricotta Cake 87
Pizza Pinwheels 165
polenta: Cheese-Stuffed
Garlic Dough Balls 163–4
potatoes: Leek, Cheese
and Potato Pie 114
puff pastry: Apricot Custard
Danish Pastries 101
    Broccoli Cheese Puffs 123
    Cherry Hand Pies 107
    Leek, Cheese and
    Potato Pie 114
    Pecan and Maple Twists 101–2
    Quick Apple Tart 103
    Raisin Swirls 101–2
    Roasted Tomato and
    Mozzarella Puff Pastry Tart 118
    Sausage Rolls 121
    Tapenade Palmiers 119
puffs: Broccoli Cheese Puffs 123
Pull-Apart Cupcake Flowers 215

Pumpkin Spiced Halloween
Traybake 207

Q

quiche: Mum's Quiche 111–12
Quick Apple Tart 103

R

raisins: Christmas Cake 178
    Oaty Raisin Cookies 40
    Raisin Swirls 101–2
raspberries: Peach and
Raspberry Cobbler 130
raspberry jam: Classic
Victoria Sponge 84
    Jam Sponge Pudding 134
recipes, scaling 15–17
Red Velvet Cupcakes 80–2
Rice Krispies: Flapjacks 41
ricotta cheese: Pistachio
and Ricotta Cake 87
Roasted Tomato and Mozzarella
Puff Pastry Tart 118
rolls: Breadgehog Rolls 166
    Breakfast Baps 151
    Fluffy Dinner Rolls 148–50
rosemary: Cinnamon Spiced
Tahini Xmas Cake 191–2
    Focaccia 158–60
    Olive Oil Cake 92
rum: Pina Colada Cupcakes 68

S

Salted Caramel-
Stuffed Cookies 49
Sausage Rolls 121
scones: Cheese and Spring
Onion Scones 93
    Classic Scones 60
Self-Saucing Sticky
Toffee Pudding 135
semolina: Cheese-Stuffed
Garlic Dough Balls 163–4
shortbread: Millionaire's
Shortbread 28
    Strawberries and Cream
    Shortbread Stacks 44
Slice-and-Bake Chocolate and
Hazelnut Freezer Cookies 43
Soda Bread 154

soured cream: Chocolate
Orange Cupcakes 195–6
Chocolate Peanut
Butter Cake 65–6
    Mini Cookies 'n' Cream
    Cheesecakes 126
    New York Baked
    Cheesecake 129
    Piñata Party Cupcakes 211
Speckled Egg Cake 200–2
spelt flour: Tomato Galette 116
Spinach and Feta Swirls 122
sponge puddings: Jam
Sponge Pudding 134
    Syrup Sponge Puddings 132
spring onions: Cheese and
Spring Onion Scones 93
sticky toffee pudding:
Self-Saucing Sticky
Toffee Pudding 135
strawberries: Easy
Strawberry Tart 104
    Strawberries and Cream
    Shortbread Stacks 44
strawberry jam: Classic
Victoria Sponge 84
    Easy Strawberry Tart 104
    Jam Sponge Pudding 134
    Viennese Whirls 46
sultanas: Carrot Patch Cake 208
    Christmas Cake 178
    Hot Cross Buns 197–9
sundried tomatoes: Olive and
Tomato Breadsticks 155
    Vegetable Rose Tarts 115
Syrup Sponge Puddings 132

T

tahini: Banana and
Chocolate Muffins 83
    Blackberry Crumbles 139
    Cinnamon Spiced Tahini
    Xmas Cake 191–2
tangzhong: Fluffy
Dinner Rolls 148–50
Tapenade Palmiers 119
tarts: Apricot Tart 106
    Chocolate Ganache
    Tartlets 98
    Easy Strawberry Tart 104
    Jam Tarts 110

Quick Apple Tart 103
    Roasted Tomato and
    Mozzarella Puff Pastry Tart 118
    Vegetable Rose Tarts 115
Tenderstem Broccoli
Cheese Puffs 123
Thumb Print Cookies 55
thyme: Parmesan and
Thyme Biscuits 56
toffee: Self-Saucing Sticky
Toffee Pudding 135
tomatoes: Olive and
Tomato Breadsticks 155
    Pizza Pinwheels 165
    Roasted Tomato and
    Mozzarella Puff Pastry Tart 118
    Tomato Galette 116
    Vegetable Rose Tarts 115
traybakes: Biscoff Brownies 75
    Cherry and Almond Cake 62
    Coffee and Walnut Squares 79
    icing 24
Pineapple Upside-Down Cake 88
    Pumpkin Spiced Halloween
    Traybake 207
    scaling recipes 16
Easy Flatbreads 161

U

upside down cake: Pineapple
Upside-Down Cake 88

V

Vegetable Rose Tarts 115
Victoria Sponge, Classic 84
Viennese Whirls 46
vodka: Christmas Cake 178

W

walnuts: Coffee and
Walnut Squares 79
whoopie pies: Mocha Choc
Coffee Whoopie Pies 38

Y

yoghurt: Blueberry
Lemon Cake 76
    Easy Flatbreads 161
    Pistachio and Ricotta Cake 87

ACKNOWLEDGEMENTS

This book would never have been possible had it not been for a stupendous team of friends and family. It's been an epic journey, and I want to thank Katya Shipster for commissioning my book – it's been wonderful working with you and the team at HarperCollins.

I wouldn't have met Katya, however, were it not for Grant Michaels at Encanta. Grant: love you big time. You are brilliant, passionate and tenacious. Thanks for everything you do! Rebecca Johnson-Honey: as soon as I met you I knew you were the one for me. I love your sassy energy and passion for what you do. Lulu Cockayne: you are a dream to work with – thanks for being SUPER organised and calming, really clever at computing and helping me through this writing process with Grant. Shout-out to Lizzie, Abbie, Joe and team Encanta. Thanks to Dominic Wood for introducing me to Encanta and for entertaining our kids and the nation for more than 20 years of course . . . BOGIES!

Endless thanks and gratitude to David Loftus, who shot this book and captured all the recipes so wonderfully. It was honestly a life goal of mine to do a book with you, David! I'm so lucky; you are such a talent and mostly a wonderful friend, with the BEST-EVER stories. Ange Loftus and the fantastic team at Fortnum and Mason for allowing us to shoot in their beautiful studio.

Tilly Hartshorn: thank goodness for you! I honestly could not have written this without you. Your work ethic, energy, style and care for the book (and me!) and the laughs. I'm so thankful. Thanks Sara De Iulio, for all your hard work and contribution – you're one cool cucumber! Thanks book crew Annabelle Davis, Kezia Osei-Adeji, Daisy Richards, Carson Thorn, Lily Hayzledon, Gina Veervaert and Aliya Kurji.

To my special being, Lydia Sear for your graph powers, the sausage rolls recipe and all your support, care and kindness. Thanks to Georgie Sear for helping with the muscle loading billions of crates and air fryers, ''avin a laff' and cheering me up! Ruby Sear: thanks for the matchas, sweet notes, jolly smile – we know, don't we!

Christine Lee, Dobby, my magical friend, for adding a touch of sparkle when I needed it – master loves you! Big love to Dan O'Malley for your help with organising my book, being a great listener, and BTS pics and videos. Thank you to Evie Radford for all the socials support!

Love and thanks to work friends who support me; my *This Morning* team, Natalie, Juliet, Kerry, Vivek, Martin and the whole crew. Lovely Gok Wan, one of THE most talented, hardworking, funniest and skilful people I know. Allison Hammond, you shine so bright and lift everyone up, and have shown me such great support. Dermot O'Leary (my baking Padawan!). Thank you, wonderful Rosana McPhee at Style Department, Rosie Shorten, Louise Sansom at FAB, Hiten Vora, Lisa Snowdon, Romy Gill, Jordan Rowley, David Obrien, Francesca Jordan, Tamsin Roberts and Jane Tyler. Triff Skepelhorn at Lolly, #TeamEgg and Clarence Court. Matt Nielsen at Nielsen Massey, Jean Egbunike. Team Kenwood, Mimi, Jo and Nadia. Kate Team Nudge PR. Trudy Monk, Emily Fella, Madeleine McCleod, Chris Corbin and the Who's Cooking Dinner x Leukaemia UK team.

Thanks to Nancy for being a superstar sister; my dad, George Walker, for always supporting and caring for me, and all your brilliant inventions. To Nanny Lydia, best mother-in-law in the world! Thanks to my oldest, special and best pal Lucy Norris – you've still got it!

Lastly, HUGEST thanks and love to Simon, my gorgeous husband, for everything you are. Thanks for always supporting me, putting up with my chaos (and seven air fryers!) and for helping me write this book, editing my jumbled text and making sense of it, for holding the fort for many months while I was on my air fryer book mission and for your strength and love. 'I'm doing it for us!'

HarperCollins*Publishers*
1 London Bridge Street
London SE1 9GF

www.harpercollins.co.uk

HarperCollins*Publishers*
Macken House, 39/40 Mayor Street Upper
Dublin 1, D01 C9W8, Ireland

First published by HarperCollins*Publishers* 2024

10 9 8 7 6 5 4 3 2 1

Text © Juliet Sear 2024
Photography © David Loftus 2024

Juliet Sear asserts the moral right to be identified as the author of this work

A catalogue record of this book is available from the British Library

ISBN 978-0-00-870977-8

Food Styling: Juliet Sear and Tilly Hartshorn
Prop Styling: Jo Harris
Design: Hart Studio

Printed and bound by GPS in Bosnia & Herzegovina

This book is produced from FSC™ certified paper and other controlled sources to ensure responsible forest management.

For more information visit: www.harpercollins.co.uk/green

WHEN USING KITCHEN APPLIANCES PLEASE ALWAYS FOLLOW THE MANUFACTURER'S INSTRUCTIONS